ENDORSEMENTS

"Iris Lavy has written a book as creative as its theme. It shows in vivid terms how the qualities of creativity, vision and willingness to break new ground by the world's greatest artists are precisely the qualities required by today's business leaders in a turbulent time of rapid and disruptive change, where old models of organization must give way to new modes of leadership and thinking. As she demonstrates, the world of art has critically important lessons to teach to world of business. This will be eye-opening for every CEO dealing with new challenges."

Ambasasdor Stuart E. Eizenstat
Former U.S. Ambassador to the European Union, Under Secretary of Commerce, Under Secretary of State, and Deputy Secretary of the Treasury in Clinton Administration (1993-2001) and Chief White House Domestic Policy Adviser to President Carter (1977-1981).

"By discussing art and leadership together, Iris Lavy has given us a brilliantly creative perspective on leadership of any kind. Anyone interested in running a team or organization, or in understanding those who do, should read this book."

Jeffrey E. Garten
Dean Emeritus, YALE School of Management. Former undersecretary of commerce in the first Clinton administration

"True leadership, like great art, is a gift. It comes from a place deep within. It is inspired by a vision no one else can see and driven by implacable passion and energy to achieve outcomes that are not negotiable. True leadership, like great art, can be unsettling. We may love its freshness or we may fear its disruption of the old order. Iris Lavy has shown us that great artists and true leaders affect us in complex ways we may not always like or understand at the time, but invariably they leave the world a richer place. We know great art when we see it and we recognize true leaders when they pass our way."

Gail Kelly
Former CEO of Westpac Bank, Australia

"Having been in several management and real leadership positions over the past 40 years, this book by Iris Lavy is a real inspiration. Highly recommended reading for people who need and enjoy understanding leadership issues for once through different lenses than management school textbooks."

Walter Kielholz
Chairman of the Board, Swiss Reinsurance
Group Chairman of the Zurich Art Museum (Kunsthaus)

"Jean Monnet, the father of Europe said "if I had to do it again I would start with culture". Iris Lavy is opening another door: art. I agree with her and wish that leaders learn from her book new ways of leading."

Maurice Levy
CEO of Publicis Groupe

"Leadership Framed by Art is unique and innovative book. Iris Lavy illuminates important topics such as vision, managing change and influence, through the use of inspiration from leading artists as well as numerous examples from the world of management. The author charts the path for future generation of creative leaders."

Galia Maor
Former CEO of Bank Leumi

"The book Leadership Framed by Art brings new life to the concept of leadership. Iris Lavy creatively weaves the principle of business leadership with insights from the field of modern art. This book is a refreshing inspiration to leaders-artists who will continue to charge the engine of creative innovation and thereby "paint the old box with new colors."

Dr. Giora Yaron
Entrepreneur and Hi-tech Industrialist

IRIS LAVY

Leadership Framed by Art

Leadership Framed by Art / Iris Lavy

Copyrights © 2017 Iris Lavy. All rights reserved.

No parts of this book may be reproduced or transmitted in any form or by any means, electronic or mechanical, including photocopying, recording, taping, or by any information retrieval system, without the permission, in writing, of the author.

Editing of the English edition by Ian Mackenzie
Proofreading by Adirondack Editing
Cover Design by Screw

Contact Info:

Email: lavy.iris@gmail.com
Facebook: lavy.iris
Website: irislavy.com

ISBN 978-1544252940

IRIS LAVY

Leadership Framed by Art

Table of Contents

Preface — 11
Introduction — 13

PART I INSPIRATION — 19

Chapter 1 THE SPOKESPERSON OF TOMORROW — 21
Manager or Leader — 22
The Leader — 23
Craft or Art? — 25
A Manager-Craftsperson or a Leader-Artist? — 29
In Short — 31

Chapter 2 MODERN ART: THE GREAT DISRUPTORS — 33
Disrupting Tradition: Damien Hirst — 35
Style Is the Content: Jackson Pollock — 36
Creative Agility: Méret Oppenheim's Furry Teacup — 39
When Materials Encounter Their Shapers: Michelangelo Meets David — 41
Looking at the Background: Édouard Manet — 43
Forging the Past: Nigel Tomm — 45
In Short — 47

PART II VISION — 49

Chapter 3 THE VISION IS ME — 51
Mapping and Identification: Journeys into Druksland — 52
Values: Ai Weiwei — 54
Adaptability and Formal Improvisation: Vassily Kandinsky — 55
Inculcating Vision: Barbara Kruger — 56
In Short — 58

Chapter 4 PORTRAIT OF A LEADER — 59
The Self-Portrait is the Message — 60
Identity: Edvard Munch — 61
Authenticity: Claude Monet — 62
A Display of Strength: René Magritte — 64
A Unique Style: Salvador Dali — 66

Managing Emotions: Vincent van Gogh	68
The Leader's Portrait in the Follower's Mirror	69
In Short	72

Chapter 5 SOFT POWER: WOMEN LEADERS IN THE WORLD OF ART — 75
Artemisia Gentileschi's Glass Ceiling — 75
Mary Cassatt's "Glass Screen" — 78
Breakthrough Female Artists — 79
Disconnecting from Female Stereotypes: Cindy Sherman — 80
Positioning "Self" at the Center: Frida Kahlo — 81
Gutsy: Georgia O'Keeffe — 82
Determination and Assertiveness: Feminism in Art — 83
In Short — 86

Chapter 6 THE FIRST BRUSHSTROKE: STEPPING INTO THE MANAGERIAL ROLE — 87
Planning According to Picasso's Guernica — 88
The Effectiveness of Focus: Caravaggio — 90
Benchmarking: Olympia Impacted by Venus of Urbino — 92
In Short — 95

PART III MOTIVATION — 97

Chapter 7 LEADING CHANGE LIKE PABLO PICASSO — 99
Trial and Experimentation: "If I Don't Look, I Won't Find." — 102
External Change: Einstein and the Dimension of Time — 103
Internal Changes: The Blue, Pink and Black Periods — 104
Courage and Professionalism: From Realism to Surrealism — 106
In Short — 109

Chapter 8 THE FOUNTAIN OF INNOVATION — 111
A Culture of Innovation — 113
Innovation: Outcome of Inspiration, or Spark of Genius? — 114
Coloring the Familiar Box with a New Shade: Henri Matisse — 115
How Simple to Simplify: Piet Mondrian — 117
Examining Under a Different Light: Claude Monet and the Impressionists — 119

Disassemble, Flatten, Reassemble: Picasso	120
Developing New Uses: Marcel Duchamp and the "Ready Made"	121
Repackaging: Christo	122
Increase or Decrease	123
Attentive to the Zeitgeist: Andy Warhol	124
The Rule is That There are No Rules: Postmodernism	126
Constructive Disruptiveness: Disruptive Changers	129
In Short	130

Chapter 9 COACHING vs. MENTORING: The two "Mona Lisa" — 131

The Leader as Mentor: "Mona Lisa"	132
The Leader as a Coach: To Grow, Like Henri Matisse	133
In Short:	138

PART IV INFLUENCE — 139

Chapter 10 THE LEADER IS PRESENT — 141

Self-image and Influence: Gustav Courbet	142
Present Leadership: A Lesson from Marina Abramovic	145
The Value of Silence: Joseph Beyus	148
Self-Positioning and Branding: Diego Velasquez and the Royal Entourage	150
In Short	151

Chapter 11 THE ARTIST'S STUDIO: EVALUATION AND FEEDBACK — 153

The Leader's Unique Voice: The Artist's Studio	155
Feedback and Evaluation: Zoom-in Zoom-out	157
Biases: Paul Klee	159
In Short	162

Chapter 12 CONFLICT MANAGEMENT MIRRORED IN ART — 163

Stretching the Shared Line: Barnett Newman	165
Creating the Harmonious Space: Mark Rothko	166
Reframing: Roy Lichtenstein	168
In Short	170
Chapter Sources	172
List of Images and Artwork Credits	177

Preface

Visual art is not a traditional source of inspiration to the business world. Art is typically viewed as something that provides esthetic pleasure to the eye and to the soul. But art is also a non-verbal narrative that allows the viewer to look, observe, perceive, and think. This is the main message of this book, that the business world can gain new insights from looking afresh at challenges and opportunities. If, as the saying goes, "a picture is worth a thousand words", then the richness of the world of art can draw a thousand colorful and creative cognitions.

In this book I attempt to link art with leadership and to draw insights from the world of art to the challenge of developing leadership skills[1]. When the idea of this linkage first came into my mind, I shared it with several friends and colleagues. I received amazing suppor from many friends who encouraged me to develop it into a modest manuscript. I am grateful to all of them and would like to use this opportunity to acknowledge constructive comments and advise from Idan Bchor, Jeffrey Garten, Stuart Eizenstat, Kathleen Hays, Gail Kelly, Walter Kielholz, Maurice Levy, Sarah Manyika, Galia Maor, Carmela Rubin, Yoram Yahav, Giora Yaron, Zvi Yemini, and Mort Zucherman. I am especially indebted to Prof. Ronald Heifetz, of Harvard Kennedy School for his extremely helpful comments and suggestions. His insights have helped me to deepen and sharpen my arguments. Finally, my deepest gratitude goes to my spouse and best friend Jacob Frenkel and my daughters, Karen and Natalie.

Introduction

THE BUSINESS WORLD OF THE 21ST CENTURY

Leadership is like beauty: it's hard to define, but you know it when you see it.

Warren Bennis

Leadership Framed by Art is meant for managers at any level to be inspired to lead. Management skills are studied in depth in business schools. The wide range of topics covers areas such as planning, marketing, and financial aspects. Today we can define fairly accurately and objectively what makes a good manager. Leadership and its definition, on the other hand, are more elusive. Can leadership be learned? Can leadership be effective without authority? How can a manager not only become an excellent shifter and mover, but also an authentic leader?

An abundance of books have been written on both leadership and art by leading experts. Leadership Framed by Art is unique for its linking of the two seemingly disparate worlds of visual art and leadership, which in this book are more like mirror images of each other. With my specialized expertise in both art history and organizational consultancy, the parallels or mirroring of these two worlds seemed logical and obvious to me. Ideas from the world of artistic creativity serve to help managers reveal the strengths encoded in their personalities, which they can then develop into leadership skills.

Artists are cultural leaders, and this is never truer than in modernity, starting with the mid-nineteenth century. Pablo Picasso, Andy Warhol, or Ai Weiwei, among many others, developed new artistic languages, spearheading change in their generations, and leading to innovative, creative ways of looking at things. Artists observe and listen to their environment, they are tuned in to the values and the perspective of their time, to than articulate in their own creative language. Like these artists, leaders leave their mark of breakthrough uniqueness on history. Vision, creativity, fearlessness, passion, and the need to create meaning should drive their work. Leaders like artists; should sit down and face the blank canvas for the purpose of sketching out the vision and the way forward.

The past few decades, and the past few years in particular, have shown the business world that the name of the game is change. The business world is shifting from an industrial economy to a digital economy. In addition to digitization, megatrends in demography, mobility, sustainability, and geopolitics are pressuring society and business. This dynamic rate of change requires a fresh and creative response. In a lecture at the May 2011 G30 Conference in Switzerland, Dr. Laura Tyson, Chair of the Clinton administration's Council of Economic Advisors and a Professor of Economics at Berkeley University, noted that one place she would not want to be at that moment was in the shoes of laptop producers. Her remark referred to the meteoric penetration of small handheld tablets into the mobile computer market. Although prophecy, as the saying goes, is placed in the mouths of the simple, Tyson's prophecy turned out to be extremely precise. By the end of 2011, it became clear that tablet sales had overtaken those of regular laptops, and that it was just the tip of the iceberg for a new trend.

Relevance, survivability, and economic growth are not givens for any business, but we are definitely in a time of opportunities for innovation and growth. Organizations wanting to maximize their inherent potential must grow excellent managers; but especially, they must grow leaders. Management has been a vital part of organizations and businesses ever since the industrial revolution, but emphasis on leadership in the business world is the outcome of no more than the past few decades. It is now clear that to lead and impact, an organization needs not only good managers but excellent leaders, and that these leaders should not only be found at the apex of the pyramid but at all levels of the organization.

Throughout human history, leaders have filled emotional roles and used their emotional intelligence skills to radiate authority and guide the organization's path. The figure of the leader aroused admiration; people looked up to the leader, from whom they drew inspiration and clarity. But in today's business arena, there is a need for a new type of leadership. One that work shoulder to shoulder with the organization's stakeholders and at the same time provides courage to embrace uncertainty and complexity[1]. Art can be a rich, powerful source of inspiration for this kind of leadership. Artists have always created in an environment of uncertainty and doubt, struggling to create with conviction and purpose. Leaders as artist can leave the comfort zone of familiar business practices to embrace new ideas and processes.

As change becomes swifter, it is vital for leaders to learn completely new skills of the kinds that are not taught in business schools. Most of the tools used for developing leadership up until recently were based on intellectual and analytical capabilities. Mike Malefakis, Associate Dean of Executive Education at Columbia University in New York, explains that innovative approaches are needed to help leaders leave their comfort zone and the usual tracks of action and thought. "In the 1990s," he writes, "the focus for executives was on analytical skills: how you as an individual can analyze data—and this remains an essential skillset for a leader to have, but it is no longer sufficient [...] now there is a new challenge, to deal with 'left-field' disruptive events that have wholly unexpected impact on a company's trading environment." Executives participating in these prestigious courses are exposed to worlds of content such as Chicago street gang cultures as researched by Sudhir Venkatesh, or urban planning as studied by Ken Jacobson, Professor of Architecture at Columbia University. Exposure of this kind expands general knowledge and assists in shaping new perceptions and ideas in developing leaders.

As a consultant and lecturer in organizations, I am in constant contact with senior and junior managers. Many feel uncomfortable in their "leader" shoes and are often unaware of the tremendous importance of a manager's ability to demonstrate leadership. Some doubt their own abilities, not believing they have the capacity needed to become a leader since, in their view, leadership is an inborn trait. Some think that being "too empowering and attentive" diminishes their authority and leaves them open to manipulation by subordinates. But my experience shows that the opposite is true. Leadership empowers managers to navigate the organization through the stormy waters of the business world. Being able to lead innovation and change, and cope with challenges, begins and ends with people. True leadership positions the organization's people at the center; it acknowledges and respects their wish for true partnership and their expectation of being involved in meaningful activities. It empowers their belief in their ability to break through their personal limitations. My work has shown me that a leader who positions employees front and center will find those employees positioning the leader front and center, and will follow that lead.

Leadership Framed by Art includes impressions from talks and encounters with top-level business and public leaders. Every year, I participate in dozens of international conferences, seminars, and workshops attended by financial and political figures who are renowned leaders in their fields—including the annual Davos Economic Forum in Switzerland. I was privileged to learn from leaders such as former US President Bill Clinton about his extraordinary ability to empower his fellow conversationalist Axel Weber, past President of the Deutsche Bundesbank and current Chair of the UBS Bank, about professional determination; Bill and Melinda Gates about social involvement; Jamie Dimon of JP Morgan Chase, about charisma and taking responsibility; Sheryl Sandberg of Facebook, about commitment to women's leadership; Jack Dorsey, founder of Twitter and Square, about leading innovative teams; Marc Benioff, founder of Salesforce about values; John Donahoe of eBay, about driving change; Jack Wiener, founder of LinkedIn, about focusing on goals; Jack Ma founder of Alibaba, about courage and boldness; and Shimon Peres, former President of Israel, about creative optimism when consolidating a vision. These, and many more, have shaped my perceptions of the essence of leadership in our current business climate.

PART I
INSPIRATION

Chapter 1

THE SPOKESPERSON OF TOMORROW

Management is above all a practice where art, science and craft meet.
Henry Mintzberg

It is commonly accepted that art represents the world of the spiritual, while business represents that of the material. Often seen as independent entities, they are actually of very similar natures. In these times of constant change characterized by complexity, the challenge of management is greater than ever. Managers are required to be leaders who actuate and inspire. Achieving growth and excellence in business means organizations must know how to switch from "managerial" modes of thinking to those of "leadership" and act boldly, with imagination, enthusiasm, and creativity. Vision, inspiration, boldness, imagination, creativity, and enthusiasm are all concepts borrowed from the world of art and creative being and doing. They are at the core of creativity but also describe the essence of leadership. Like the artist, the leader operates from a deep need to contribute and create. Leaders as artists are visionaries. They draw on their unique personality, values, and the ability to react to their environment. By that, they can arouse creative energy, inspiration and focus abilities of distinction, self-expression and out-of-the-box thinking.

Manager or Leader

Dr. John Kotter, Professor Emeritus at the Harvard University Business School's school of leadership, published an article in January 2013 in the Harvard Business Review blog noting, "Management is not (yet) leadership." He explains how, even after four decades of teaching and consultancy to business companies, he frequently encounters confusion over the two terms "management" and "leadership." He cites three common errors:

1. People swap one term for the other indiscriminately, without relating to the importance of each function separately.

2. Many tend to think that leaders are at the peak of organizational hierarchy, and management is the next level down.

3. People tend to think charisma is vital if you want to be a leader. Charisma derives from the Greek for "divinely gifted grace." But since those blessed with such grace are few and far between, Kotter claims that the assumption is unfounded. Were it true, then logically almost no one could become a leader.

Management, says Kotter, is a set of known actions such as planning, budgeting, setting teams for specific operations, measurement and control, and problem-solving. Management is how an organization produces the products and services it has committed to at a uniform quality and within a balanced budget on a daily basis. In large organizations, management is complex and challenging, and extremely important.

Leadership is not the same as management. Leadership is something else altogether. Leadership thrusts the organization into the future. Leadership identifies current opportunities and where they are headed so that the organization can realize its potential. Leadership links vision and the people who empower that vision. More than all else, leadership leads change. In our world of fast-paced change, there is room for more and more people with the ability to lead.[1]

The difference between a manager and a leader can be viewed from many perspectives. Professor Ronald Heifetz, the Co-Founder of the Center for Public Leadership in the Harvard Kennedy School, view leadership as "motivating people to do adaptive challenges." According to Heifetz, organizations face technical problems and adaptive challenges. In times of crisis people look for authority (the manager? I.L.) to guide them. But "leaders do not need to know all the answers. They do need to ask the right questions." Technical issues require authoritative expertise (the manager? I.L.), and can be solved. Once solved, the conditions are likely to resume to their original state. Adaptive problems, on the other hand, are systemic problems with no ready answers. "Adaptive work is required when our deeply held beliefs are challenged, when the values that made us successful become less relevant, and when legitimate yet competing perspectives emerge." Since there are no ready answers to adaptive challenges, the leader must refer to its people to "feel the pinch of reality" and to do the adaptive work. The leader needs to mobilize people to embrace change and to learn new ways to deal with the changing needs.[2]

The speed of technological change and economic change has set a challenge to every organization. "When the cost of employing development engineers in China and India is one quarter of the cost in Israel, the risk that these functions will shift from Israel to the Far East seems more tangible than ever," stated a headline in the Israeli business newspaper.[3] Far East employees hold a clearly quantitative advantage, and were raised on a culture of obedience and diligence. Israel's main advantage is its human resources, which excel in creativity, resourcefulness, and innovation. To continue driving these three traits, and continue coping with a world of fast-paced change, managers need to develop and employ their leadership skills.

The Leader

Managerial professions are studied in depth in business colleges. Managers focus on processes and should excel at planning, organizing, financing, and strategy implementation. The role of managers is to execute tasks effectively, while that of the leader is to focus on people and change, to look toward the future, and to inspire others to follow the path of change. The leader is in fact tomorrow's spokesperson who drives unique and authentic vision into opportunities.

Leadership is an acquired ability and an inseparable part of management. A person may be a great manager, but not every great manager is necessarily a leader. How can leadership be "taught?" How can managers be turned from excellent implementers into inspirational leaders who light the spark of motivation and innovation in their employees? Just as the graduate of an art school does not become an accomplished artist overnight, the manager or business management college graduate does not automatically become a leader.

Studies encompassing more than 100,000 leaders of diverse organizations throughout the world and published in *How to be exceptional: Drive leadership by magnifying your strengths* proves that organizations need leadership at all levels. The researchers pointed to the advantages of leadership:

- Leaders draw talent, because others like them want to work with them.

- Leaders assist employees in discovering the latter's latent abilities and producing the best they can. Quality teams develop into creative cooperation.

- Leaders tend to stay in an organization in order to build themselves, others, and the organization itself. They promote stability and confidence.[4]

Organizations wishing to thrive need both managers and leaders. Henry Mintzberg, Professor at McGill University in Quebec, Canada, and a founder of modern management principles, claimed that many in the worlds of academia and business have fallen in love with the concept of leadership, and many managers aim to be outstanding leaders. But separating the two, he claims, introduces a certain risk. Management without leadership leads to uninspired execution of tasks, whereas leadership without management encourages a dissociated style and excessive confidence with destructive potential.[5]

Craft or Art?

Art has described and recorded culture throughout human history, and has duplicated reality (mimesis). The Italian Renaissance of the thirteenth to sixteenth centuries was the golden age of art, with its rebirth of classical culture. Renaissance artists of that period documented Christian and mythological scenes. For the first time in centuries, artists once again attained the technical skills to sculpt rigid cold materials such as marble into shapes as supple, breezy, and glossy as silk, or imbue the flat canvas with depth and distance based on the laws of perspective. The excellence shown by artists of that time is measured to a great degree by their technical capability, their craft—or, in other words, their skill at describing and documenting the object or topic with as convincing realism and precision as possible. The greatest of this period's artists, such as Leonardo da Vinci or Michelangelo, distinguished themselves at their craft and, in return, earned personal fame.

Baroque, Rococo, and the Romantic periods followed the Renaissance period heel to toe but none brought great change. The artists' technical skills were worthy of great praise, yet the artists continued working within the accepted norms, usually satisfying their patrons' demands. The artistic activity was conducted according to fixed, exacting rules. Recurring endlessly are scenes depicting religious and mythological themes or portraits of the artists' patrons, all in a technically accepted and uniform style. The artist himself (almost all of those known to us being male) had little impact on the nature of the work or its content. Most often, the artist did not create in order to express himself or portray an idea, vision, or message, but because that was his work and source of livelihood, and usually a meager one at that. Baroque, Rococo, and Romantic period artists do have a place in the history of art, but according to the perspective of modern art, they were more craftsmen than artists. "They viewed themselves as craftsmen, good workers whose learning never ends. At that time, the objective of art had not yet been invented, nor had the path of the genius, the all-knowing individualism, and other vanities. You needed to be in control of your work, and put it to decent use."[6]

From around the mid-nineteenth century, artists sought to free themselves from the art academy's rigid, dictated rules, which set a hierarchy of subject matter and techniques for creating art. Claude Monet was a leader in the revolution that came to be known as the Impressionist movement. His unique approach brought about the birth of modern art as we know it. Impressionist artists were without doubt affected by the cutting edge technological development of those times invented by Louis Daguerre in 1834: the camera. Because it took perfect likenesses, the camera freed Impressionists from focus on the craft to focus on vision and artistic expression. **In Water Lilies** (image 1), Monet presents a reality as he sees it in real time under the existing lighting conditions, as opposed to artists of the generation preceding him who painted according to what the viewer was educated, and ex-

Image 1: Claude Monet, *Water Lilies*, 1919

pected, to see. With short brushstrokes, vibrant pure colors, and thick texturing, Monet gave no accentuation to details. These elements made the painting seem "unfinished," almost like a full color sketch. For subject matter, the artists drew on everyday life or topics close to their hearts, expressing their new visions boldly and courageously. Monet and his fellow Impressionists led a conceptual and creative revolution and brought into being a new, authentic world of visual art.

Impressionist paintings, mingling virtuosity with innovative techniques, took the artistic institutions of the time by storm, shaking their foundations. Opposition from art institutions, and a public that bowed to the institutions' unanimous voice, made no difference to the artists. Determined, persistent, they eventually earned the status of pioneers of the new artistic era known as Modernism.

Modernism, with its multiple streams, celebrated the revolutionary, the artist's ability to create and achieve, and opened the gates of the world of art to cultural renewal. Leading artists in the modern world were, in fact, the cultural leaders of their times, and are still considered cultural icons in ours. They were the founders of breakthrough schools of thought, spearheads of conceptual, ideological, and aesthetic change. Impressionists freely expressed their stances as a way of voicing the artist's uniqueness instead of complying with the demands of the customer or patron. By rejecting anachronistic views held by academic art institutions, and ignoring the barriers they encountered, Impressionists forged a new artistic language, altered the face of the art world forever, and were the catalysts of additional changes well into the future by generations that would continue to speak in terms of art's new reality.

A Manager-Craftsperson or a Leader-Artist?

Organizations in current reality need the conceptual change of a kind similar to that experienced by Modernism in art. Adapting itself to an array of changes, the organization must move from actions focused chiefly on technique and skill to original thinking that turns raw materials into unique creations. Organizations must aspire to move away from the craft that drives their activity and duplicates familiar templates, to the art of their activity, based on vision, inspiration, and innovation. The technological and informational revolutions of our current times not only created new infrastructures for organizational transformation but also serve as that transformation's catalyst. Smart business leaders create opportunities that take advantage of these new infrastructures. They use them to springboard the organizations into a constantly renewing, innovating world.

As the professional fluent in the organization's activities and goals, the business manager wears the craftsperson's hat. The leader, who drives the vision and change, wears the artist's beret. The world of management began developing simultaneously with the industrial revolution, responding to a growing need for ways to control increasing numbers of employees. Business organizations were manufacturing institutions that adopted the assembly line approach to quickly produce uniform items. Assembly line workers were the craftsmen. No creativity was called for. Their whole function was to produce.

Most of the management theories with which we are familiar were developed at the outset of the twentieth century, their espousers having been born around the late nineteenth century inspired by the steam engine industrial revolution. The theories were formulated around manufacturing organizations governed by management norms that, much like art patrons of those and earlier times, dictated rigid criteria to the factory or manufacturing plant workers. The nature of assembly line work required developing expanded management skills but still very little in the way of leadership skill. This style of management went from the sweatshops of early Victorian mills to Henry Ford deciding to pay his line workers $5 a day—a large sum at the time. By the end of the twentieth century, the mass-produced uniform assembly line item was being replaced by custom tailored products, serving to the preferences of a consumer living in times of abundance. The fourth industrial revolution, inspired by the massive technological developments, is already taking place to alter the business world once more. Advanced robots, for example, as can be seen in Amazon packing and delivery systems and the 3-D printing industry are already leaving their mark on industries.

Volatility, Uncertainty, Complexity, and Ambiguity (VUCA) characterize today's world. In this competitive and ever-changing business environment, the need for vision-inspired leadership is greater than ever. Leadership that will embrace and develop innovation and creativity, that will serve to bring employees' commitment and involvement to new heights. Organizations need both managers and leaders. However, organizations that are incapable of identifying the difference between leadership and management will find it difficult to realize their fullest inherent potential. Leaders infuse their vision through their behavior, inspiring the organization and its employees. In this way the leader shifts away from the role of "foreman," or craftsperson of the old world, into that of the artist leading employees and the organization, rousing creative and emotional energy of the kind needed by a dynamic company.

The current business world is replete with lavish monuments to once leading organizations that lost their position in the technological tsunami washing over them. One of the most noticeable is the former photography giant Eastman Kodak, which did not identify the impact of digital photography on their core business—the film camera. Interestingly enough, it was Steven Sasson, an engineer at Kodak, who invented and built the first electronic camera in 1975. In the 1990s, Kodak planned a decade long process to shift to the digital technology, but the company failed to anticipate how fast digital cameras were becoming a commodity. Nor did Nokia manage to optimize its control over the mobile phone market in Europe and the Far East to lead the development of smartphones based on touch screen interaction. These huge companies were perhaps involved in duplicating successful templates of the past, wreathing their own brows with the laurels of success. Kodak and Nokia are examples of companies that continued doing what they did yesterday and the day before but forgot to look ahead, toward tomorrow.

One leader who did look ahead was Steve Jobs, the legendary founder of Apple and the person who infused color, touch, and passion into the technological age. Under

Jobs's leadership, Apple realized the ultimate link between art and craft, between uncompromising execution and breakthrough vision. Apple's products and tools over the past decade, such as iPod, iPad, iPhone, iTunes, and iCloud, have changed the face of technology beyond recognition. Apple was able to create such products because, as Steve Jobs explained, "we always tried to be at the intersection between technology and the arts." This is the underlying creative approach at the launch of every new Apple product. Jobs's vision was to create and develop the most amazing thing possible, then go even further. He encouraged his employees to think and behave like artists and aspire to break through boundaries that limit creativity. It is no wonder that the boardrooms at Apple's offices in Palo Alto, California, bear the names of breakthrough artists such as Leonardo da Vinci or Pablo Picasso.

As technology continues to disrupt industries, businesses need leaders that are pioneers who depart from conventions like the Modernists in the art world. They need to prevail and lead the challenges of the algorithmic-based environment. Nowadays, Uber has turned the smartphone into a tool, which dramatically affects pricing, and the availability of car rides, throwing the traditional taxi business into turmoil. The Uber phenomenon is one of the most important economic movements. As Nassim Taleb, author of The Black Swan and Antifragile tweeted: "To 'Uberize,' to remove the middleman, theme of the times." This on-demand service under the fingertips of consumers is threatening the entire economy and the fear of "Uberization" of everything is a common concern and challenge.

In Short

- In times of fast diverse change, organizations need leadership at all levels.

- Every manager must also be a leader. In the business world, the manager is the craftsman and the leader is the artist.

- A leader, like the artist, is driven by and drives vision, passion, and self-expression.

- Leaders and artists draw their abilities and power from their environment and personal paths of development.

- A leader must first and foremost be able to manage and lead themselves.

Chapter 2

MODERN ART: THE GREAT DISRUPTORS

You have got to get people to listen to you before you can change their mind.
Damien Hirst

What common denominator links Mark Zuckerberg, founder of Facebook, and one of the greatest of the twentieth century's artists, Pablo Picasso? What do the artist Damien Hirst and Jeff Bezos, founder and CEO of Amazon, share? At first glance the obvious answer is "nothing," but there is far more in common between them than meets the eye. Art and leadership are two of the most observed disciplines, but they remain the least understood phenomena. Questioning "What is art?" can be paralleled by "What is leadership?" Neither question can be answered unequivocally. We generally identify both leadership and art intuitively.

Artists are among the greatest disruptors of culture and human thought. They undermine existing norms and conventions while working under great uncertainty. In their work, they oppose blindly kowtowing to preset rules to promote cognitive and conceptual flexibility and freedom. Their innovative and bold artistic statements are the outcome of deep emotional engagement and passion. They dare to challenge conventions and to express their vision to reach new and unique visual languages. Artists are cultural leaders who invite their peers to join them as they break through boundaries and plow forward.

Image 2: Damien Hirst, *Anatomy of an Angel*, 2008

A work of art is the product of head, heart, and hand. In other words, it represents an investment of thought (intellect), emotion (passion), and technical ability (the craft). Effective leadership is also an integrated triangle of intellect, passion, and craft. The leader's objective is to bring about a chain of actions and reactions that will drive organizations and employees, much as the artist wishes to drive the observer of an artwork to feel and react. The leader seeks to arouse the employees emotionally and intellectually in order to inspire commitment and to imbue even routine actions with a sense of meaning and purpose. Professor Nancy Adler is an artist and a management professor at McGill University. She also serves as a management consultant to international corporations. In an article published by her she asks: "Now that we can do everything, what will we do?" This question becomes more relevant than ever with the passing of time. Adler emphasizes the connection between the world of business and the world of art as a source of inspiration encouraging out-of-the-box thinking, connecting to emotion, firing enthusiasm for creativity, and allowing self-expression.[1]

Disrupting Tradition: Damien Hirst

Damien Hirst's **Anatomy of an Angel** (image 2) is a provocation to a sculpture by Alfred Boucher titled *Woman Washing*. More than a century spans between the two almost identical works. Yet Hirst presents an innovative version: he scoffs at the myth of idealized feminine beauty and exposes the woman's internal organs, her guts, as a way of bursting her angelic image and turning her into mere flesh and blood. Sometimes "you have to kill things in order to look at them," said Hirst[2], one of wealthiest and most successful living artists that the history of art has ever known.

A similar line of thinking led to the establishment of Southwest Airlines. Herbert (Herb) Kelleher, a pioneer of low-cost flight, looked deep at the guts of the aviation industry and discovered new realm of possibilities. Kelleher founded Southwest Airlines in Dallas, Texas, in 1971 and served as CEO for many years. The company started operation with just four jets but still was able to fiercely battle the established large airline companies. Initially, the company ran the one-hour flights from Dallas to Houston at a cost of $10, halving the price offered by its competitors. Southwest offered the following services: none. There were no meals, no reserved places, and no higher-class seating. Kelleher competed on the basis of price alone. In fact, he stripped the airline product of its service elements in order to position Southwest not only as a worthwhile alternative to other flights, but also as a viable alternative to travel in private vehicles or other public transport. Kelleher actually disrupted the airline industry as we knew it. In 2011, some 135 million people had taken the company's flights, revenue had reached $15 billion, and the company reported profits of $179 million. Unlike every other airline in the world, Southwest has never recorded a full-year loss and has only lost money in a single quarter in its history. Excellent service as far as scheduling and competitive pricing in particular gave Southwest Airlines the edge over competitors as clients turned it into the most favored airline in the US. Like Hirst, Kelleher looked at the existing model of traditional airlines, and provided a new translation of the model by opening up cheap flights, on limited but popular routes flying out of second-tier airports.

Style Is the Content: Jackson Pollock

Managers differ in their personality and their work style. Some managers are more oriented toward people and others may be more oriented toward tasks and results.

Professor Ichak Adizes studied the different types of managerial style in depth. In his book Management/Mismanagement Styles: How to Identify a Style and What to Do About It, Professor Adizes lists four distinct types of managers and how each one's managerial style impacts the way the role is fulfilled.

According to Adizes, the first is the results-oriented manager, the second is the administrator, the third is the entrepreneur, and the fourth is the integrator who coordinates the different internal parts of the organization, and its activities, with other external parties. Adizes outlines each one's character traits and enumerates each one's advantages and disadvantages. The author also describes the managerial style best suited to the organization's life cycle, or stages of development. Adizes's management styles theory indicates that every manager has strengths and weaknesses and no one can excel in all four parameters. Since every organization needs all four styles, his recommendation is to structure a team where each one's personal style covers the organization's different roles and needs.

From Adizes's management style theory it is clear that a leader's personal management style will impact the organization's nature and conduct. The work of the artist Jackson Pollock could shed a light on the relations between the work process and the outcome. Pollock's artwork is an embodiment of his style; his technique is the content. Pollock's work style is often called "drip art" or "action paintings" because of the nature of the work. Pollock set his canvas out on the studio floor and moved around and across it, flicking and dripping paint straight from the can onto the canvas. This dynamic technique expressed his essence as a creator of artwork; no preparatory drawing or plan is involved in his work.

The energy of the free-flowing movement of his body, combined with liquid paint, allowed the paint to drip and swirl naturally, layer after layer. Pollock is physically present in the painting. His entire body and being are partners to the work being done. Pollock himself stated, "I feel nearer, more part of the painting, since this way I can walk around it, work from the four sides, and literally be in the painting."[3]

In the same way, leaders who bring their creative and dynamic energy and move in and around the organization have a great effect. They are able to create a unique composition by actually being present in the picture. Such leaders are likely to find out that working side by side with employees enhances teamwork, improves decision-making, and contributes to organizational agility.

If a good definition for Pollock's art is "action painting," then an equally good definition of Mark Zuckerberg's style is "action leadership." The approach of "move fast and smash things" typifies and reflects the culture that Zuckerberg, founder and CEO of Facebook, assimilated. Zuckerberg absorbed the ethos of hackers from Silicon Valley but took this culture to empowered levels with the unique Facebook culture.

Most technology companies operate under controlled conditions where new products are given a beta run before hitting the general consumer market. But not Facebook (FB)—the company usually does not run beta versions. Instead it runs a set of products and tests on real-time users. Even before FB trainees have completed their six weeks of learning and assimilation in the company, they are working on the live site and get to see the whole code base. This style of management can cause mistakes, but Zuckerberg "can live with that" because, as far as he is concerned, the most important thing is to learn on-the-go. The faster the company learns, he believes, the faster the company will reach its optimal model. Without doubt, Zuckerberg's style impacts content: at the end of 2012, FB showed a remarkable one billion users.[4]

As leaders, style or mode of operation can shape the culture, norms and values the organization. Style of leadership can be manifested in different ways; such as the way meetings are held, customer are served or decision are made. Just as there are diverse styles in art, there are different personal styles of management. A leader operating in the Cubist style, which views objects as geometric planes, may demonstrate the ability to abstract or be able to identify and map templates, people, and situations. A leader who functions in a Surrealist style, which is the expression of the dream-state or the subconscious, is the entrepreneurial and visionary leader. These concepts are not the work of behavioral science or artistic research but an attempt to consider how diverse styles impact results and outcome. A leader's personal style is of great importance—the "how" will result in the "what."

Creative Agility: Méret Oppenheim's Furry Teacup

No artistic talent or know-how is required of managers in the business world, but in a world of frenetic pace of change, creative agility is vital for coping with conceptual or structural challenges. Infusing creative agility into organizations means linking strategy to execution and implementation.

In artists, uncertainty has always been a catalyst for experimentation and creation. The work of Méret Oppenheim (image 3) is one example of solutions to challenges that use unconventional materials. The link between fur and the teacup is surprising, and at first sight arouses our aversion. But precisely that kind of agility and out-of-the-box thinking stirs the interest factor in this work.

In the business context, the same question can be raised. What materials or processes can be used that will allow new products and industries, even though they may seem unfeasible? What can still be done that has not yet been done?

Image 3: Méret Oppenheim. *Spoon, saucer, fur cup.* 1936 © 2016, ProLitteris, Zurich

Out-of-the-box thinking and agility, rapidly and creatively adapting to changes and emerging opportunities are the name of the game. Products that were until recently considered science fiction are now possible. Impossible Foods Inc. is a Bio-Technology innovative company that its claim to fame comes from creating the first real meat experience made from plants only. It is a lab-derived meat patty that looks and tastes exactly like real beefy hamburger. This new hamburger is already served in top restaurants in New York and is receiving great feedback. It is not only satisfying a growing community of vegans but it is also supporting sustainability. According to livestock researchers, animal agriculture creates the equivalent greenhouse effect impact of the entire global transportation system combined. Impossible foods have made the impossible possible, and when it comes to using unconventional materials in business, it is just the tip of the iceberg.

When Materials Encounter Their Shapers: Michelangelo Meets David

Brush and paint, marble and metal, are some of the components used by artists. Employees, clients, shareholders, the company, and the organizational environment are the components through which the leader operates. The famous marble statue of **David** sculpted by Michelangelo Buonarroti is 17 feet tall. The marble was quarried from Carrera, Italy, some 40 years before Michelangelo produced the sculpture. Two other sculptors, Agostino di Duccio and Antonio Rosselino, had previously attempted to work with the same chunk of stone but, it is said, they ceased their efforts due to insufficient experience on their part, and what was claimed as the raw material's poor quality.

Talent such as that of Michelangelo, who was able to create a magnificent work despite whatever faults the raw material possessed, parallels that of leaders coping with complex challenges. For Michelangelo, the beauty was already embedded in the stone; he only needed to expose it. This is exactly the task of the leader, to enable people to discover their abilities and inherent potential.

In business, a world where the overall components of organizational activity—such as suppliers, human resources, client loyalty, and product success—are subject to the leader's authority, is a fantasy that rarely comes true. Drawing the best from them all requires high levels of skills in both leadership and management.

Image 4: Édouard Manet, *Portrait of Emile Zola*. 1868

The same organizational components can bring one leader to success and another to failure. Just as artists learn all they can about the materials they are planning on using before beginning their work, so leaders must deeply familiarize themselves with the organization's products, culture, environment, clients, and employees. This lets them identify when breathing room is needed, when specific actions are required, when innovations should be empowered, and when to exert authority.

Apple, the extraordinary computer company, can be likened to the block of marble that Di Duccio and Rosselino failed to sculpt, whereas Steve Jobs in the role of Michelangelo produced magnificence. In 1997, when Jobs took over the reins of Apple for a second time as its chair and CEO, the organization was in a sorry state, suffering huge losses and with its very future in doubt. In August 1997, he announced the signing of a strategic cooperative agreement with Microsoft, Apple's bitter long-time rival. With this decision, Jobs rescued Apple from its niche player status in the technology market and began repositioning it as a giant. In January 1998, Jobs was already announcing a modest quarterly profit. Following years of losses, the profit had the aura of a true miracle. In 2012, Apple had the highest market value of any company in the United States, proving that business failures do not necessarily prevent a talented leader from leading an innovative vision.

Looking at the Background: Édouard Manet

Sometimes "what is essential is invisible to the eye" wrote Antoine de Saint-Exupéry in The Little Prince. Indeed, observation of an artwork usually focuses on the figures, objects, and subject of the work, while background is given secondary importance. But frequently enough, the background is what allows the viewer to discern the topic.

In the portrait of the author Emile Zola painted by Édouard Manet (image 4), the background overflows with information that the artist wishes to convey to the observer. Zola holds a book in both hands. On the table is an inkwell ready for writing. This makes it easy to deduce that the man whose portrait is being painted is a man of the written word, without us knowing for a fact that he is an author. On the wall behind him, Manet has "hung" a Japanese print to explain his own source of inspiration and that of an entire generation of artists of his time. An even smaller painting on the wall of Zola's room is a replica of Manet's own Olympia, portraying a nude woman inspired by the goddess of love, Venus, even though she was alleged to be a prostitute. Olympia was criticized harshly by the artistic-academic establishment of Manet's time. None of the background details in this painting are coincidental; they are an inseparable part of the painting's topic. By checking the background carefully, Manet tells the viewer that Zola, like himself, is a revolutionary and fellow norm-breaker.

In November 2011, Bank of America published an announcement that it would collect a fee of $5 per month from credit card holders starting in 2012. The public outrage surprised the bank so much that it was forced to backtrack and dump the plan long before it got underway. The bank's management simply ignored the "background music," the mood of the public, at the time. Following the 2008 financial crisis, opposition by a large percentage of the American public to all things bank-related was written on the wall in huge, blinding letters. Organizations have to operate within social, economic, technological, and political backgrounds, which are part of the whole picture for organizational activities. Organizations never operate in a vacuum, and the multiple facets forming its environment must be given consideration before leading change.

Some will claim that differentiating between that background and the central goal is artificial, but they are in fact completely interwoven with each other. The bottle of ink, the Japanese prints, the figure of Olympia, and Zola's portrait merge together into one creative image with the clear message, just as business decisions—such as the level of bank fees—must merge completely with the prevalent economic climate which, in this case, includes the social revolution in the background. Had Édouard Manet focused only on the central goal, being the portrait of Emile Zola, his own world would have remained hidden and the image would lack a context. Art buffs would have missed out on one of the most majestic works Manet produced.

Forging the Past: Nigel Tomm

People in general, and artists in particular, fall in love with their own concepts and the works in which they have invested their time, thought, and effort. But sometimes an artist needs to know when to let the work go and bid it farewell. This is the reason that the work of the contemporary photographer and writer Nigel Tom is especially captivating. Every work produced by Tomm is like a photograph crushed before being thrown into the trash. Tomm purposefully crumples the images—making them seem almost disposable. It appears as if Tomm erases or crushes all of the works that do not meet his expectations.

Occasionally, even the most wonderful, creative ideas do not integrate into a "big picture," and despite the challenge they hold artists know when to "wipe out" their work in order to preserve these bigger picture concepts.[5] The artist, as a professional authority, is the one to decide the fate of the work.

Leaders, like artists, must also know when to stop and cut short or discard a process or project that does not meet its budget, priorities, or expectations. A leader must apply due consideration and professional authority when making such decisions. Sometimes an excellent idea that is not implemented at the right time or pace relative to market conditions can become outdated and economically not viable.

Dov Modan, one of Israel's hi-tech industry founders, developed the "disc on key," more commonly known as the USB flash drive, and turned it into an incredible success. The company under which it was made, M-Systems, was bought by SanDisc for some $1.6 billion. In 2007, Modan established the Modu company. It developed a compact mobile phone, which took top place as the most lightweight cellular phone on record. It offered few functions, as a kind of core of the much larger cell phones. The uniqueness of Modu was in its ability to be matched to various envelopes that would supply the user with experiences according to user need. The innovative idea seemed promising, but in the end, the company did not survive, failing to raise the funding needed to go public. Absorbing heavy losses, the company went into bankruptcy in 2010.

But Modu's failure could have been identified at the outset of its path. In 2007, when Modan established the company, Apple launched its first iPhone, which took the cellular / mobile phone market by storm. The market conditions created by the penetration of such an innovative item left no room for yet another innovation in the same field. In interviews Modan gave after the company folded, he admitted that the question of why he did not forgo the idea when he should have continued to echo in his mind.

Giving up on an idea can actually open up the horizon to new opportunities. Out of the big bang and collapse of Modu, totaling $120 million in losses, some 30 start-ups came into the world, begun by former Modu employees, including Modan himself. The experience, vast know-how, and emboldened business acumen gained at Modu became the fertile ground for developing and implementing other new ideas.[6] These companies produced hundreds of work places and technological applications that brought new value into the market.

In Short

- Leadership, like art, breaks through the boundaries of its time in order to drive creative change.

- Herbert Kelleher and Damien Hirst realized that "sometimes you have to kill something in order to see it."

- Impossible Food and Méret Oppenheim demonstrate the same kind of flexible thinking, which realizes creative ideas.

- Steve Jobs and Michelangelo produced magnificent works despite the limitations of the raw materials available to them.

- Jackson Pollock's and Mark Zuckerberg's personal work style is characterized with dynamism and energy. Their works manifest that style can also create content.

- The background is an inseparable part of the overall picture, as can be seen from the portrait of Emile Zola, or the activities of the Bank of America.

- Like artists, leaders and businesses must know when to give up on an idea that seems good on the page, but for various reasons does not work in reality.

PART II
VISION

Chapter 3

THE VISION IS ME

The leader never lies to himself, especially about himself.
Warren Bennis

Leadership success begins with vision. Vision is most often described as a mental image or picture that outlines a desired direction and a path that the organization wishes to attain. Leaders who have brought their organizations to realize their full potential fused their personal vision with that of the organization. The two are tightly related and complement each other.

Leaders, like artists, are visionaries. They infuse people with the courage to imagine the unimaginable. Their mission is to help people define direction and purpose by questioning and listening.[1] To do so, leaders must define their own identity and values that drive them. They must be clear on who they are and the direction they are taking before raising similar questions with others—questions such as: "Who are we?" (Identity) or "Why do we exist as a group?" (Purpose and significance). As with the artist, leaders must draw a sweeping picture of their vision that when converted into words will sum up the mutual direction and purpose for each member of the organization. Standing before that picture, observers will try to read its messages. In the business world, these "observers" are employees, clients, and any other groups of people involved with the organization.

Mapping and Identification: Journeys into Druksland

Leaders' values and personality are an integral part of the organizational image. Daniel Goleman, author of Emotional Intelligence and co-author of The New Leaders, claims that revealing and exposing the "ideal self" is of vital importance to shaping the image of the leader and manager one wishes to be. A leader operating from within her or his personal vision toward realizing the self brings excitement and passion to the work being done, and draws subordinates into operating with the same passion and enthusiasm.[2] Defining personal vision means diving deep into the personal psyche to identify and map internal sources and values.

Artists commonly use sketching, painting, and sculpting their self-portraits as a means of learning and exploring their own essence and nature as individuals and artists. The self-portrait produced by Michael Druks (image 5) blatantly demonstrates this search. Druks adopts the format of a topographic printed map that identifies and represents land conditions, to map his own portrait. This is, in fact, the subtext of his artwork. The work's title, Druksland, indicates the search for self and reinforces the message. Druks does not attempt to produce a physical likeness to his real visage, but describes the internal process of searching and identifying meanings concealed within himself.

Managers are surrounded in their workplace by diverse sources that can assist with making the organization's decisions. Many leaders nonetheless mention "loneliness at the top." The source of this feeling is because, at the end of the day, the decisions and responsibility for their outcome rests on their shoulders. Leaders must be deeply aware and able to evaluate their own abilities if they wish to cope successfully with responsibility. Honest assessment will strengthen their professional decision-making and empower their commitment to their path and vision. Viewing the self-portrait of a personal vision as a tool for self-learning and self-definition is being more frequently applied in modern companies. Meetings of senior man-

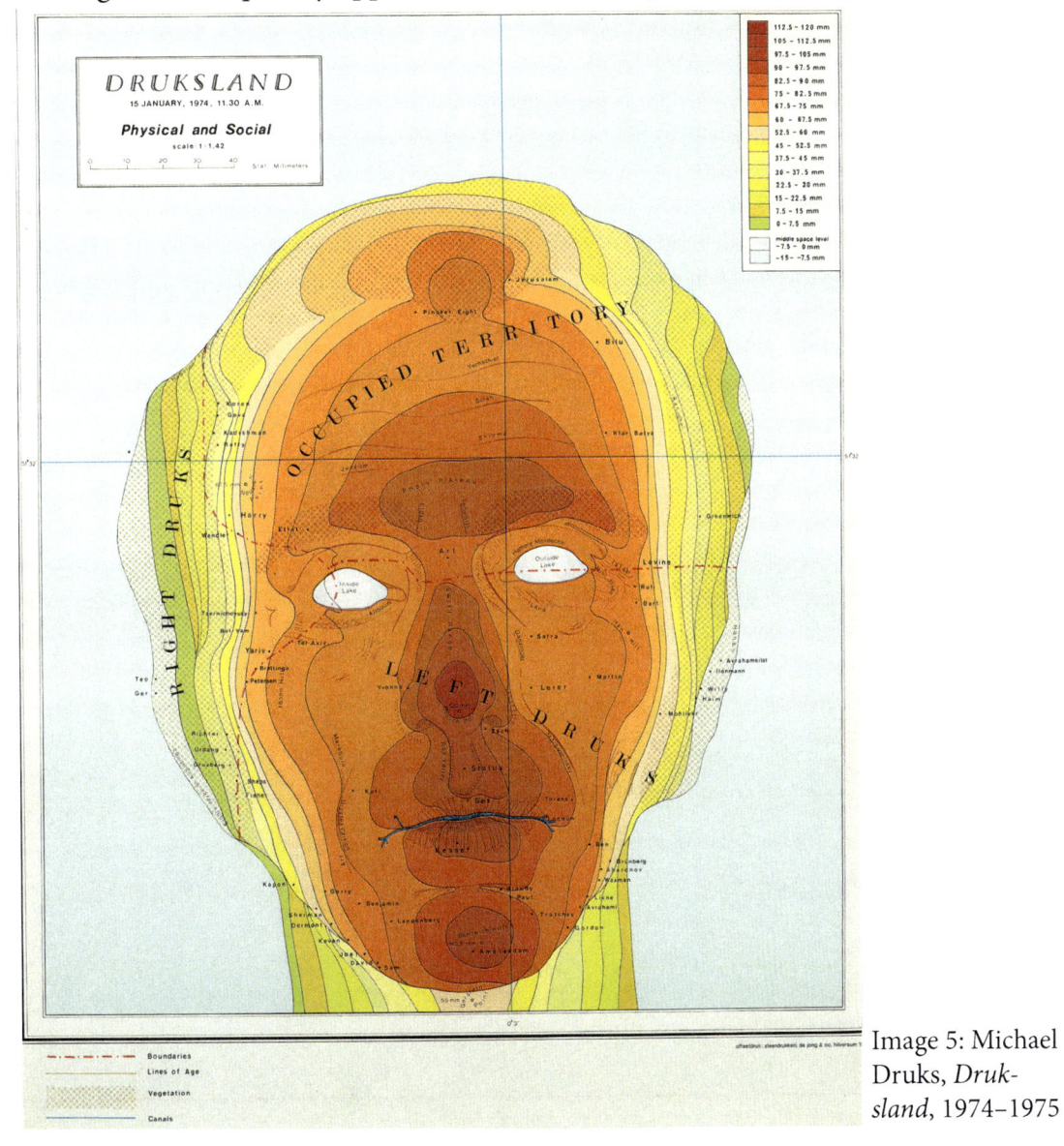

Image 5: Michael Druks, *Druksland*, 1974–1975

agement for strategic discussions are now often held over long weekends, outside of the office environment, which turns them into an important avenue not only for consolidating the management team, but for each member of it to define her or his personal self-portrait, which in turn will project the company's vision.

Values: Ai Weiwei

Leaders need to articulate their core values, those that cannot be compromised. These are the foundation of the journey toward becoming a leader and will guide the way when the road gets rocky. The Chinese contemporary artist Ai Weiwei makes daring works unlike anything the world has ever seen. In 2011, the editors of ArtReview magazine named him the most powerful artist in the world. The tremendous respect and success that came to Ai Weiwei is much due to his leadership as a human rights activist in China. His artistic work is provocative and brave, a manifestation of his uncompromising values as a human rights activist and leader. Although he was arrested and restricted from leaving China, Ai Weiwei was determined to express his view and criticism. In many of his works, he challenges the Chinese government on issues such as corruption, lack of transparency, human rights, and freedom. After the devastating Sichuan earthquake in 2008 that left over 90,000 people dead or missing, Weiwei led a team to survey and film the post-quake conditions in the disaster zones. He discovered that the collapse of 20 shoddily constructed schools caused the death of many schoolchildren. He clamored for the government to admit that corruption had enabled the builders to ignore safety codes when erecting the schools, and asked to publish the names and the tally of the children who perished. In his work **Straight**, he produced a 38-ton installation constructed from rebar collected from the collapsed schools.

He employed craftsmen to heat and then straighten each piece of quake-twisted steel, manually restoring them to their pre-disaster condition. The work Straight is accompanied by a list of the 5,192 names of children who perished. In his blog, he wrote, "This investigation will be remembered for generations as the first civil rights activity in China. So, to me, that is art. It directly affects people's feelings and their living conditions, their freedom and how they look at the world."

"As a leader, who you are is more important than what you do,"[3] said Frances Hesselbein, summing up what she learned from the man described by BusinessWeek magazine as "the man who invented management." Ms. Hesselbein is Chair and founder of the Frances Hesselbein Leadership Institute. It was founded as the Peter Drucker Foundation for Non-profit Management. Leaders stand out because of their personal values that project onto the organization and are reflected both in their actions and words.

Adaptability and Formal Improvisation: Wassily Kandinsky

Wassily Kandinsky, a pioneer of abstract art and color theory is one of the leading artists of the twentieth century. His work over the years is the culmination of both formal study and free improvisation. The music education as a child, the law and economics studies, the interest in psychology, and the research of color and form were instrumental to his vision as an artist. In 1912, he wrote his first book, *Concerning the Spiritual in Art*, which laid the foundation to the theory of abstraction. Kandinsky's deep analytical research of pictorial elements led him in 1926 to write the book *Point and Line to Plane*. His wide knowledge and thorough study enabled him to develop visionary and playful works. Many of Kandinsky's works titled Compositions have a free and improvised nature and surprisingly, works titled Improvisations have a formal structure, a kind of "formal improvisation". This is well portrayed in a work such as *Composition VII* that appear improvised while a work such as *Improvisation 7* that maintains a formal structure.

In today's complex and dynamic business world, there is a need to adapt to a vision that is "formal improvisation." The combination of the terms formal and improvisation might appear contradictory at first. As it was introduced and practiced by Kandinsky, a formal composition is planned and programmed and at the same time has the ability to deal with the unexpected and unplanned by improvising in real time. Vision improvisation is not about pulling a quick fix out of your sleeve but rather, it is based on deep understanding and analytical study of the market challenges and the organization internal values and strengths. To the business leader it means adaptability. This process of improvisation and adaptability is widely apparent in start-up companies that embark on a journey with a conceived vision but the dynamic reality forces a shift and a change of direction.

Inculcating Vision: Barbara Kruger

The works of conceptual artist Barbara Kruger convey a clear message. **I Shop, Therefore I am** (image 6) is a protest against consumer culture. Kruger, who began her professional career in magazine design at Mademoiselle, takes advantage of her familiarity with the world of design, marketing, and mass media by employing their images and symbols to express her strong stances on consumerism and social climbing. Kruger sets her vision and beliefs before the observer with direct and bold messages that are easily absorbed and use sharp, unfussy design elements to stay content-focused.

Image 6: Barbara Kruger, *Untitled (I Shop Therefore I am)*, 1987

In the business world, leaders too can infuse inspiration through a simple statement to express vision, mission, and values. Leaders who seek to inculcate their vision must express it in direct, relevant, easily assimilated, and precise form. A good example is WeWork, a company that was established in 2010 by two young entrepreneurs, Adam Neuman and Miguel McKelvey. The company provides shared workplace and services for entrepreneurs, freelancers, start-ups, and small businesses. The mission of the company is "To create a world where people work to make a life. Not just a living." The company's name is in itself the message and the vision—to transform the Me into a We, to create a community. The simplicity and the directness of the title are combined with relevance to the values of the company's audience. It uses a language that speaks to the heart of global trends such as connectivity and to the values of Generation Y. WeWork was named one of the most innovative companies of 2015 by Fast Company magazine. It has since evolved their mission to WeLive (2016), a similar concept to WeWork in shared residential housing, and in 2011 to WeLab that serves as a start-up incubator.

In Short

- Organizational vision is the "big picture."
- Leaders like artists are visionaries who impact the organization vision.
- Consolidating personal vision begins with mapping of the self.
- Personal vision reflects values as can be seen from Ai Weiwei's works.
- Vision adaptability is about drawing a formal improvisation.
- The vision must provide direct, focused, and easily assimilated messages like those of Barbara Kruger.

Chapter 4

PORTRAIT OF A LEADER

My idea of a group decision is to look in the mirror.
Warren Buffett

Opportunities to lead are found all around us, but the ability to lead is deep inside us. True leadership arises from internal human resources and, as such, cannot be taught in a conventional way. There is no blueprint or magic solution by which one becomes a leader. At times, circumstance may open up a chance to lead; in other cases, the leader grows into the role through a conscious choice and the personal motivation to develop. Usually, attaining leadership is an upwardly spiraling process of internal observation, learning curves, and self-recognition. The first person that the leader leads is her- or himself; only then can the leader sweep others up into their leadership.

David Novak, Chair and CEO of YUM Brands, managing 1.4 million employees in 117 countries worldwide, claims in his book, *Taking People with You*, that success as a leader begins with self-awareness, also known as "Just be yourself." Part of the difficulty in being ourselves is due to the fact that we do not know who we truly are, especially in the early years of our career. The business outcomes of Novak's management testify to the fact that he learned about himself and his abilities thoroughly—between 2003 and 2012, YUM Brands showed consistent growth of 13 percent per year.[1]

Managers aiming for sweeping leadership must first look themselves straight in the eye and sketch their desired portrait as a leader. In the world of art, the passion to solve and refine the mystery of the self has, for centuries, led artists to draw their self-portraits. It served as a visual dialogue with the self and a self-learning mechanism. The self-portraits portray in a subjective manner the uniqueness and the essence of the self. Artists mold those raw materials of the self into an image. The image can then become a map for further investigation of the self. The artist Ofer Lalouche explains the effect of his self-portraits on him: "The fact that I research myself always changes me, which then requires further research."

Leaders must first look themselves straight in the eye and sketch their desired portrait as a leader. In the world of art, the passion to solve and refine the mystery of the self has, for centuries, led artists to draw their self-portraits. Self-portraits are, in many cases, an act of humility since it is about soul-searching and self-questioning. It is a visual dialogue with the self and a self-learning mechanism. The self-portraits portray in a subjective manner the uniqueness and the essence of the self. Artists mold those raw materials of the self into an image. The image can then become a map for further investigation of the self. The artist Ofer Lalouche explains the effect of his self-portraits on him: "The fact that I research myself always changes me, which then requires further research."

Leaders like artists aim to create a dialogue with their public, and the messages being conveyed by their self-portraits have tremendous value. Each viewer can see something different in the self-portrait, but in fact each viewer is actually seeking, and therefore identifying with, something of her or his own self in the artist's self-portrait.

The Self-Portrait is the Message

Studying the self-portraits of diverse artists shows the direct affinity between these works and their overall collections. A consistent message weaves its way like a silken thread between the image portrayed in the self-portrait and other works by the same artist, even if those are in different genres such as landscapes or still lifes. The language in which the artist expresses the self-portrait is identical to that used in other works. This language noticeably conveys the artist's nature, identity, val-

Image 7: Edvard Munch, *Self-portrait with Cigarette*, 1895

Image 8: Edvard Munch, *The Scream*, 1893

ues, and vision. This is very much the same with leaders. Their definition of their "self-portrait" as leaders will directly affect their organization and people. Let us examine how the message in self-portraits is manifested in the grand picture.

Identity: Edvard Munch

Self-portraits by Expressionist movement artist Edvard Munch, for example, convey to the observer feelings of isolation, loneliness, and anger (image 7). Munch uses the same content language as that appearing in paintings of other subjects. In his famous work The Scream (image 8), a terrifying scream breaks through the inanimate canvas, and the observer cannot help but sense the harsh emotions. How the artist perceives himself as seen in his self-portrait is paralleled by his personal style in general; we could say the totality of his work is, in fact, a portrait of his personal identity.

In the January 2013 edition of the Harvard Business Review, listing the world's 100 top business leaders, Jeff Bezos was slotted in second place and topped only by Steve Jobs. Bezos founded and chaired Amazon since its inception in 1996. Amazon's value under Bezos's leadership was listed at $111 billion. The company's share spiked an astonishing 12,266 percent between the company's establishment and the end of 2012.

Bezos explains his success as an entrepreneur with a phrase that defines his identity as a leader: "I believe you have to be willing to be misunderstood if you're going to innovate."[2] This statement was made against the background of doubt voiced by his competitors over the surprising service he wished to provide to clients, sometimes with no profit to the company. Customer centricity is a core value identified with Bezos, who allows clients to publicize critical feedback on his products on the company's website. Bezos sold the Kindle device without any evident profit. His willingness "to be misunderstood" defines his identity as a leader and, as such, influenced Amazon's culture that puts the client first and operates on the basis of a long-term business mindset.

Authenticity: Claude Monet

Claude Monet, a founder of the Impressionist movement, believed that art should reflect the artist's everyday life in its natural setting. Accordingly, artists should leave the gloomy studio's four walls behind in favor of natural light when documenting those everyday scenes. Monet pioneered this concept, giving rise to the movement's name based on of one of his works, *Impression, Sunrise*. As befits his authentic vision, *Monet's portrait*, painted by his colleague Édouard Manet, serves as an example for viewers and artists of his generation. Manet places secondary importance on Monet's facial outlines and instead focuses on the message he feels is more important: documenting the image of the artist in the open air, in the floating studio, under conditions of natural light. Indeed, all of Monet's works, such as the *Water Lilies* series, dealt with methodically recording nature under changing conditions of light. He painted the water lilies some 250 times in order to identify and record the impact of light on them at different times of day and different seasons of the year, and painted dozens of other subjects repeatedly, in series, where natural light is the differentiating factor. Monet became a leader to his contemporaries and for the generations to come due to the authentic commitment to his vision.

Authentic leadership is built through honest and ethical foundations. Authentic leaders are genuine and lead from the heart. Marc Benihoff, founder and CEO of

SalesForce.com, is a great advocate of social responsibility and philanthropy. His company's employees are encouraged to give back to their communities and the company matches the employee's gift, dollar for dollar, up to $5,000. Benihoff not only advocates and encourages but also actually walks the talk. As of 2016, he had contributed $100 million to various institutions in the San Francisco area, mainly to the children's hospital, UCSF, and the public school system. Benihoff pioneered a philanthropic model one-one-one, by which companies contribute one percent of profits, one percent equity, and one percent of employees' hours to their community. This model was adopted by many other companies[3].

A Display of Strength: René Magritte

Inner strengths are a focal layer in the ability of any one person to drive and lead others. Looking at the self-portrait of the renowned Belgian artist René Magritte (image 9), we see how he zooms in on his own internal strengths. Viewers can infer his self confidence, fastidious grooming, and elegance. His internal focus of power is so strong, as painted on the canvas, that from just one glance he is able to derive the image of the dove from the egg resting on the table.

Because he is able to see what will spring from the egg before the fledgling has even hatched, Magritte clarifies to the viewer a self-awareness of his unique powers and uses them well. His self-perception as an individual with extraordinary qualities, as portrayed in this and other self-portraits, is a theme running through all his work. In **The Treachery of Images**, (image 10) the painting conveys a mixed message: on one hand, Magritte paints a pipe with amazing perfection, but on the other hand, the French caption tells us "This not a pipe." Magritte's personal strengths as re-

Image 9: René Magritte, *The Clairvoyant* 1936

Image 10: René Magritte, *The Treachery of Images*, 1929

65

flected in his artwork allow him to produce the reality that he feels is correct. These are clear leadership traits. Leaders must be able to identify their abilities and power and set their conceptual paths with focused determination. If leaders cannot rely on and believe in themselves, why should employees believe in them?

Jack Ma, founder of the Chinese online behemoth Alibaba, was chosen as the Financial Times 2013 Person of the Year. A combination of factors explains their decision to choose him. The scope of sales conducted by the organization, established by Ma in 2003, is far greater than eBay and Google combined. Its share issue in 2016 set its value at more than $250 billion. Ma retired from his role as the company's CEO and chair at the end of 2013 in order to devote his time and funds to rehabilitating China's environment and water.

Ma represents the new Chinese entrepreneur, a person who began as a poor child and becomes such an admired business leader in China that the admiration borders on worship. At the party celebrating the company's first decade of business, the enthusiastic voices of 16,000 employees cheering "Ali Alibaba" thundered around the Hanzu sports hall where the function was held. Ma's tremendous power could be identified right from the company's start. He invited 17 people to his apartment, spellbound them with a sweeping speech, and stated that "Chinese brains are just as good as theirs, and this is the reason why we dare compete with the Americans. If we're a good team and we know what we want to do, then one of us can defeat ten of them."[4] Ma's power, much like that of Magritte, derives from his ability to look into the egg and, with foresight, know what will be hatched. This is how he led a gargantuan public to believe in him.

A Unique Style: Salvador Dali

Salvador Dali, the Spanish artist, is most commonly recognized for his unique flamboyant personality, relentless self-promotion, and that famous moustache of his. In his work, Dali sought to free the mind and human awareness from the constraints of rationality, creating a dreamlike language that gives self-expression as much freedom as it wants. His work is a vivid representation of unforgettable dreamscapes depicting an inner surreal world. His tireless curiosity, talent, and extraordinary imagination led him to engage deeply at different phases in his life with contemporary science, religion, mysticism, and popular culture. But it was Dali's eccentric personality and unique style that made him one of the leading figures of the art scene in the twentieth century.

A personal style and uniqueness as a leader are sourced in inherent self-knowledge; only then can a leader build the skills and practices needed. A unique personal expression empowers the leader to embed that uniqueness in the organization. Richard Branson, founder of the Virgin Group and its CEO, is a charismatic, colorful leader. He began his journey in 1975 as the owner of a small recording company in London. By 2012, he headed some 200 companies under the Virgin label, including Virgin Airlines. How the airline came into being says more than a thing or two about Branson as an innovative, creative entrepreneur. In 1975, as a young man, he wanted to fly with American Airlines from Puerto Rico to the Virgin Islands. At the last moment, American Airlines canceled the flight due to unprofitability. Branson was not about to despair. He hired a small plane at the airport and wrote on a large sign: "One way to Virgin Islands $29." He sold all the places in no time, and the experience led him to purchase his company's first jet, named for the first destination to which he organized a special charter.

Branson explains his success as a combination of presence, creativity, and prominence, which differentiated him from competitors and labeled the Virgin Group (and himself) as being unique. Creating prominence requires, in his view, that leaders be distinguished from others, to garner headlines, and to cause the public to familiarize themselves with the product. Fun, courage, and innovativeness are the key words in the culture Branson inculcated at Virgin. A great example of his colorful personality can be found in an early 2012 event. One day, at 5.30 a.m., he was informed that the enormous Ferris wheel known as the London Eye and sponsored by British Airways, Virgin's bitter competitor, could not be erected due to some technical problem. In the blink of an eye, Branson called up the airship company he owned, sited just outside London. Next thing, a huge blimp was seen floating over the Ferris wheel with the bold message: "British Airways Can't Get It Up."[5]

Like Salvador Dali, Branson lets go of all constraint and gives full rein to his creativity. Actually, there is no way to differentiate between the leader and the company. The face of Virgin Group is the face of Sir Richard Branson.

Managing Emotions: Vincent van Gogh

Vincent van Gogh is known for saying he wanted to "paint what I feel and feel what I paint."[6] In his self-portraits as in most of his works, such as **Starry Night**, he passionately passes on to the viewer the swirl of powerful emotion. With circular movements, blatant colors, and short furious brushstrokes, van Gogh brings the viewer into the whirlpool of feelings and emotions in order to share the narrative of his agitated spirit. As can be seen in his work and understood from his statement, he was aware of the emotions flooding him. His tragic end by suicide indicates that he failed to effectively manage his internal storm.

A leader's reaction and emotion are examined under a magnifying glass, requiring that leaders examine and choose the degree to which they externalize emotion. This does not imply that leaders must always wear a poker face and allow nothing to show, but too much emotion will most likely undermine the organization and cause subordinates to lose their confidence and sense of stability. Rudolph William Louis "Rudy" Giuliani III was chosen as Time magazine's 2001 Person of the Year for his confident, calm management of New York City as its mayor during the 9/11 Twin Towers terror attack. Despite the catastrophic event and the sense of expanding crisis felt throughout the city, Giuliani's message and image set a confident tone and helped get life in the Big Apple running as smoothly as possible, as quickly as possible.

The power of leadership lies in realizing personal skills and emotional awareness. Emotions are crucial to building trust, engaging and forming close ties with people. By managing their emotions, leaders can effectively respond to people and to situations. Just as van Gogh's emotions were not hidden from view in his paintings, a leader's emotions are manifested. Like the artist, the leader should look at the colors on the palette and choose the shade of emotion that optimally expresses their message.

The Leader's Portrait in the Follower's Mirror

Leadership receives legitimacy from followers willing to be led and motivated. Political leaders understand the impact of their image on public opinion and use it to their benefit. Alexander the Great was the first to receive expansive public recognition by imprinting his portrait on a coin, an act that later became commonplace worldwide. The first Roman emperor, Caesar Augustus, successfully reinforced his role as a politician and leader by positioning himself throughout the Roman Empire in the form of statues glorifying his image.

The artists who painted the portraits of great leaders in history were actually subordinates subject to the leader's rule and whimsy. The organization is a reflection of its leading figure; there is clear significance to the way in which subordinates perceive the leader's image. Napoleon Bonaparte's portrait for example, created by the French artist Jacques Louis David in the early nineteenth century, glorifies the leader and his achievements. Up until the era of modern art, which started around the mid-nineteenth century, artists would elaborate on and empower the leader's image—whether deserved or not. The goal, of course, was to broadcast a message of strength, power, and influence. These portraits were usually ordered by the emperor, by royalty, or by patrons who wished to glorify their leader or themselves. Napoleon's portrait (image 11) reflects his tightly controlled autocratic leadership—a man who makes unilateral decisions.

Starting at around the twentieth century, artists used these portraits as a means of expressing their views on the leader—to protest the leadership, express support, or criticize the leader's image and actions. In the modern world, artists don't generally serve as the leader's trumpet but instead express the way in which they perceive a leader. The portrait of US President J.F. Kennedy was immortalized by the Pop artist James Rosenquist in a collage titled **President Elect**. The work has popular products of the times pasted around Kennedy's portrait, seemingly without any connection. Included are a package of instant cake mix and an American vehicle. In this way, the artist presents the president as yet another consumer item marketed through populist media, a brand like all brands. Embedded in the work is

Image 11: Jacques Louis David, *Napoleon Crossing St. Bernard*, 1800

defiance of the American myth of consumerism and commercialism.

These examples of leaders' portraits are rife with symbolism. Sometimes they demonstrate the artist-subordinate, and how the leader is perceived and that leader's messages. Other times, these artists express political, cultural, and social nuances drawn from their environments, in the portraits. The observer can identify different meanings, both overt and covert. To a very great degree, the leader's portrait is influenced directly from that leader's values, commitment, messages, and personal example as shown to her or his subordinates. The portraits of Napoleon and Kennedy were admittedly produced in different countries and different historical eras, but both broadcast a clear opinion about their roles as leaders from the artists' viewpoints.

"Leadership is the art of getting someone else to do something you want done because he wants to do it," said former US President Dwight D. Eisenhower.

Leadership has many hues. As with artists, who study their self-portrait to learn the about the contour and the nature of themselves, leaders can also choose how to flesh out their images and reflect their "ideal selves." Leaders who clearly define themselves and their vision, nature, and character of their own image radiate this onto the personal and professional conduct of their subordinates.

In Short

- Leadership is a choice.
- Like artists, leaders should draw their self-portrait and map out the "ideal self."
- Drawing a self-portrait is an intellectual process to learn about the self.

- The leader's portrait is the message. It projects onto the organization.

- Leaders can sketch their portraits to reveal:

    » Self-identity like Edvard Munch and Jeff Bezos.

    » Authentic self that will radiate outward like Claude Monet and Marc Benihoff.

    » Sources of inner strength and power like René Magritte and Jack Ma.

    » Unique style like Salvador Dali and Richard Branson.

    » Skillful emotion management like Vincent van Gogh and Rudy Giuliani.

Chapter 5

SOFT POWER: WOMEN LEADERS IN THE WORLD OF ART

Leadership belongs to those who take it.
Sheryl Sandberg

Art reflects and documents the reality of its time. Close observation of the art world therefore reveals the microcosm of women's status in society. The fingers of one hand suffice to count the number of women who were formally trained as artists up until the nineteenth century. Art as an occupation was considered suitable only for men. Women who painted were generally considered as doing so only for their personal pleasure or to flaunt their potential value as wives. Attitudes changed in the twentieth century, chiefly due to the feminist revolution. Currently, it is more and more that artists, both men and women, are judged on quality of the work rather than on the gender of the creator. How did it come about that such a change of status occurred in the world of art relative to women, from total disregard to fully contributing and being recognized as equals?

Artemisia Gentileschi's Glass Ceiling

Women painted and sculpted throughout history, and some were highly skilled but rarely achieved fame. The names of Michelangelo and da Vinci and their works are household names, but few have heard of Artemisia Gentileschi or Marietta

Robusti, who painted during the Renaissance period.

Women during those times were not permitted to be involved in art as a profession, and those we do know about were required to paint in an artists' studio owned by a male family member. Although women are currently free to take part in any activity, within that freedom they frequently encounter gender inequality known as the glass ceiling, a term popularized in the 1980s to describe a transparent barrier that blocks women who are climbing the public or corporate ladder. The glass ceiling may have come into being from an erroneous perception of the "ideal leader" as male—powerful and assertive, authoritative and competitive in a world where social conventions viewed the woman's primary role as the backbone of family.

In the world of management, a company wanting relevance in the market must reflect reality. The company or organization's business activities must derive from a broad range of people representing reality: women, men, minorities, and people of different religions. This is indeed a breakthrough, but it can't compensate for the minuscule representation in business top management. In mid-2016, Kevin Roberts, the chairman of advertising agency Saatchi & Saatchi, was encouraged to step down from his position after delivering a sexist statement about women in his organization. He said that he did not consider the lack of women in leadership positions a problem for the advertising industry and he continued: "I am just not worried about it because they are happy, they're very successful and doing great work." This remark led to a storm of criticism and shed light once more on the astounding lack of gender disparity in an industry where 50 percent of all employees are women while only 11 percent are in leadership positions.

Study after study shows that gender diversity contributes to positive business out-

Image 12: Cindy Sherman, *Untitled* #92, 1981

comes, but still only about 20 women could be identified as holding key roles of president or chairperson for the largest organizations in the USA. Among them are prominent business leaders such as Meg Whitman, President and CEO of Hewlett Packard; Marissa Mayer, President and CEO of Yahoo; and Mary Barra, CEO of General Motors. Despite corrective legislation and even though more than half of all students for advanced degrees are women, their representation in senior management and boards of large public organizations still does not match their numbers as a percentage of the population.

Mary Cassatt's "Glass Screen"

The glass ceiling is often the proverbial fig leaf concealing the glass screen. The glass ceiling currently referred to is not the only barrier women face when seeking to fulfill their professional potential and develop into leaders in their fields. In the mid-nineteenth century, Paris was the heart of the Western art world and there, too, women were very poorly represented. Men could devote themselves to art. They were the ones who fashioned the direction of its development, change, and revolutions. Women were usually left with the traditional roles of wife and mother, and their art focused chiefly on handicrafts such as embroidery and sewing. The rare few who entered the artistic pantheon during that period, such as Mary Cassat or Berthe Morisot, were indeed very talented artists, but they painted topics with a "female focus," unlike their male colleagues whose spectrum of topics was far wider.

In their works, Cassatt and Morisot documented women who spent their time reading books in the garden or embroidering or dealing with housework. Their manifestation as artists is drawn from the home as the context and content. As such, the home served as "glass screen," through which women could gaze at the world. In retrospect, it seems that they wish to be part of the fabric of business and public life, but in fact many of them avoided stretching out a steadfast hand and simply taking hold of the opportunities in their professional environments.

Women surround themselves, consciously or unconsciously, with "glass screens." Being transparent, it is not visible but it is extremely powerful. No one marks out the position or territory of women other than women themselves. They are the ones who define their own boundaries. Defining this glass screen is not easy, since each woman has her own screen, so to speak. The glass screen's existence is due to multiple and complex reasons but include social and cultural norms, education, convenience, fear, absence of skills for achieving in the "man's world," or skills for coping with achievement. The glass screen separates women from their goals and dreams of self-realization.

Breakthrough Female Artists

By contrast to the business and public sectors, the status of women in art gradually reached equality with that of men. As noted, artists are now judged chiefly on the quality of their work rather than their gender. The twentieth century feminist revolution and the unique nature of art offered women the chance to stride into the heart of a world considered male for a very long time. Art produces critical thinking, and it questions, examines, and defies. The artist Sigal Landau describes her artistic activities as a passion deriving from an inner voice. Artists' self-expression is the outcome of vision, determination, persistence, talent, and self-realization. Women artists who have broken through and opened the path to other women for generations to come simply did not allow the glass ceiling to stop them in their tracks. Instead, they shattered it.

Developing skills and the ability to lead require breaking through both the glass ceiling and the "glass screen." Women in the business world can adopt role models from the world of art who were cultural leaders by virtue of their activities. Cindy Sherman, Frida Kahlo, Georgia O'Keeffe, Judy Chicago, and Barbara Kruger are just some of the many women who broke old conventions and altered norms in modern art. They led a cultural revolution with passion and courage to pursue their self.

Disconnecting from Female Stereotypes: Cindy Sherman

When a man gets up to speak, people listen then look. When a woman gets up, people look; then, if they like what they see, they listen. So said the Hollywood actress of the 1930s, Pauline Frederick. And not much has changed since then. Women are still measured by their external appearance. Wishing to examine female stereotypes, Cindy Sherman (image 12) photographs herself in sequences. She appears in staged situations, in diverse costumes and outfits, each time presenting herself as a different female figure. She gives no names to her work, but numbers them. In this way she hopes that any woman can find herself in the photographs.

Sherman raises questions about the way women are perceived in society, and how this perception shapes their images. To a great degree, the "glass screen" is the outcome of how society shapes the image of women, and the high threshold of expectations our culture expects of women. This same threshold circles back to impact the image of women and therefore defines women's sense of self-esteem and their status in society. In a 2012 retrospective held in New York's MOMA (Museum of Modern Art), Sherman displayed wall-size photographs after seeing art shows by male peers. She had been thinking big, producing murals printed on a kind of contact paper. She got the idea, she said, after seeing how "a number of male artists would get invited to do a show somewhere, and they'd just fill up an entire wall of painting that is just this gigantic thing." She added: "I was thinking how pretentious that is. It made me realize not too many women artists think that way."

Positioning "Self" at the Center: Frida Kahlo

Behavior that seems fitting to men is said to involve "doing," whereas that suited to women is usually described as "providing" or "nurturing" and is always directed toward, and inclusive of, others. Women tend to devote the best years of their lives to caring for family while simultaneously positioning themselves on the lowest rungs of their scale of priorities.

Women account for 50 percent of the global workforce, according to the United Nations report, while men's participation is at 77 percent.[1] Although women contribute to the family's income, the attitude toward their professional activity is still viewed more as "work" and less as "career." In many families, it is women who need to give up a day at work to attend their children's needs. Positioning the self center-stage invites opportunities to crack that "glass screen." This means that women need to put their wishes and ambitions in the center as well. Realizing their professional potential and building leadership abilities requires that women believe in their capabilities and act with commitment and determination to realize their vision and aspirations. To position themselves centrally, as Frida Kahlo did.

The bulk of Frida Kahlo's work deals with self-portraits, which is also what makes her unique. Kahlo (1907–1954) put her "self" at the center of her artwork and almost all one hundred of her works are devoted to searching, examining, and expressing this self. In fact, one of the questions motivating her artwork is "Where am I?" Kahlo, who contracted polio as a young child, suffering a slight and manageable impediment, was also critically injured as a teen in a freak tram accident in Mexico City. The injury from the tram accident left her unable to become pregnant. She painted her portrait repeatedly, embellished with various symbols including animals that perhaps express her desire for the children she could never have, or images that describe her barrenness such as the typically male haircut with the lopped-off hair scattered about.[2]

Kahlo fearlessly described her tormented body after the harsh accident she suffered, and realistically expressed her disappointment with her body's inability to bear children. Her openness, determination, and methodical focus on herself as a person and a woman turned her weakness into her strength. Kahlo is a fascinating example of a woman who developed into a symbol of charisma and leadership, and her works are admired by many, especially women.

Gutsy: Georgia O'Keeffe

A true pioneer of twentieth-century American art, Georgia O'Keeffe (1887–1986) grew up in a time when women artists had no opportunity to express themselves openly and directly without being viewed as coarse and even wanton. O'Keeffe remained an independent woman even after her marriage, never hesitating to be bold, to do and say as she felt and wished at the personal and artistic levels. In the conservative society of the early twentieth century, she presented a new, personal, direct approach of a kind no woman had yet dared to try.

O'Keeffe painted large-scale abstracted flowers that radiated power and sensuality. Some viewed them as blatant sexual symbols. O'Keeffe admittedly refused to authenticate these interpretations, but her paintings and conduct were a clear statement of female boldness and independence breaking through boundaries. Her male peers praised her work as the best of women artists in her time, but she waved the compliment away, saying that she aimed to be the best of artists in general, not merely relative to other women.

Georgia O'Keeffe may not be perceived as a woman ruled by fear, but in a journalistic interview, she noted: "I've been absolutely terrified every moment of my life and I've never let it keep me from doing a single thing that I wanted to do."

Determination and Assertiveness: Feminism in Art

Feminist artists operating in the 1970s in the USA brought about deep social changes in all areas of life, and particularly in the world of art. Their belief in their chosen paths, their sense of entitlement toward their abilities and their bodies, and a respect for women's achievements were part of the messages conveyed in their work. The artist Judy Chicago's installation titled **The Dinner Party** is an important icon of 1970s feminist art and a milestone in twentieth-century art. The Installation integrates handicraft usually tagged as having a female nature, such as embroidery, sewing, and ceramic painting. The dinner table perpetuates the names of 39 women leaders in their fields, and 999 more women's names are integrated into the ceramic floor tiles. By placing significant women around the table, Chicago's work is a protest against the Western male art traditions in which significant men are seated around the table, such as in da Vinci's The **Last Supper.**

Barbara Kruger, on the other hand, used her work to protest violence against women and supported the woman's wish for control over her body, including the option of abortion (image 13). The statement these women artists make is that women are not born to behave in a womanly fashion but have been socially and culturally instructed to believe they should. With their statements, they assisted an entire generation of women in bringing about a change in awareness that cracked the proverbial "glass screen."

Women in the world of art succeeded because they refused to let fear prevent them from breaking through the glass ceiling, nor were they captives to remaining behind their own glass screens. They directly and boldly chased their dreams and challenged the world managed by men alone, believing that there was no other way to create. Over the long journey still remaining, in which women must remove the glass barriers, it is women who must take an active part and contribute to bringing those barriers down.

One of the reasons for the disparity in income earned by men and women for the same position in the business world, according to research conducted by the economist Linda Babcock of Carnegie Mellon University, is that women simply do not ask for a raise whereas men, acknowledging their self-esteem (or even without consciously acknowledging it), set a price for their skills that they think is fair. Babcock's study was published in 2003 in her book, *Women Don't Ask*. Since then, little seems to have changed. Women, on average, earn less than men in virtually every occupation as full-time workers. The Latest OECD report shows that women earn about 15 percent less than men, while in the USA the gap is at almost 18 percent. Research published in the "European Journal Work and Organizational Psychology" studied the effect of agreeable behavior versus dominant behavior of both men and women on wages. The research found that "dominant" men were at the top of the wage chart and were followed by the "agreeable" men. "Dominant" women earned less than the "agreeable" men and last came the "agreeable" women.[3] Acknowledging the right of women to equality will only occur when women themselves show confidence in their abilities and stand up for their rights with assertiveness and determination.

Image 13: Barbara Kruger, *Untitled (Your Body is a Battleground)*, 1989

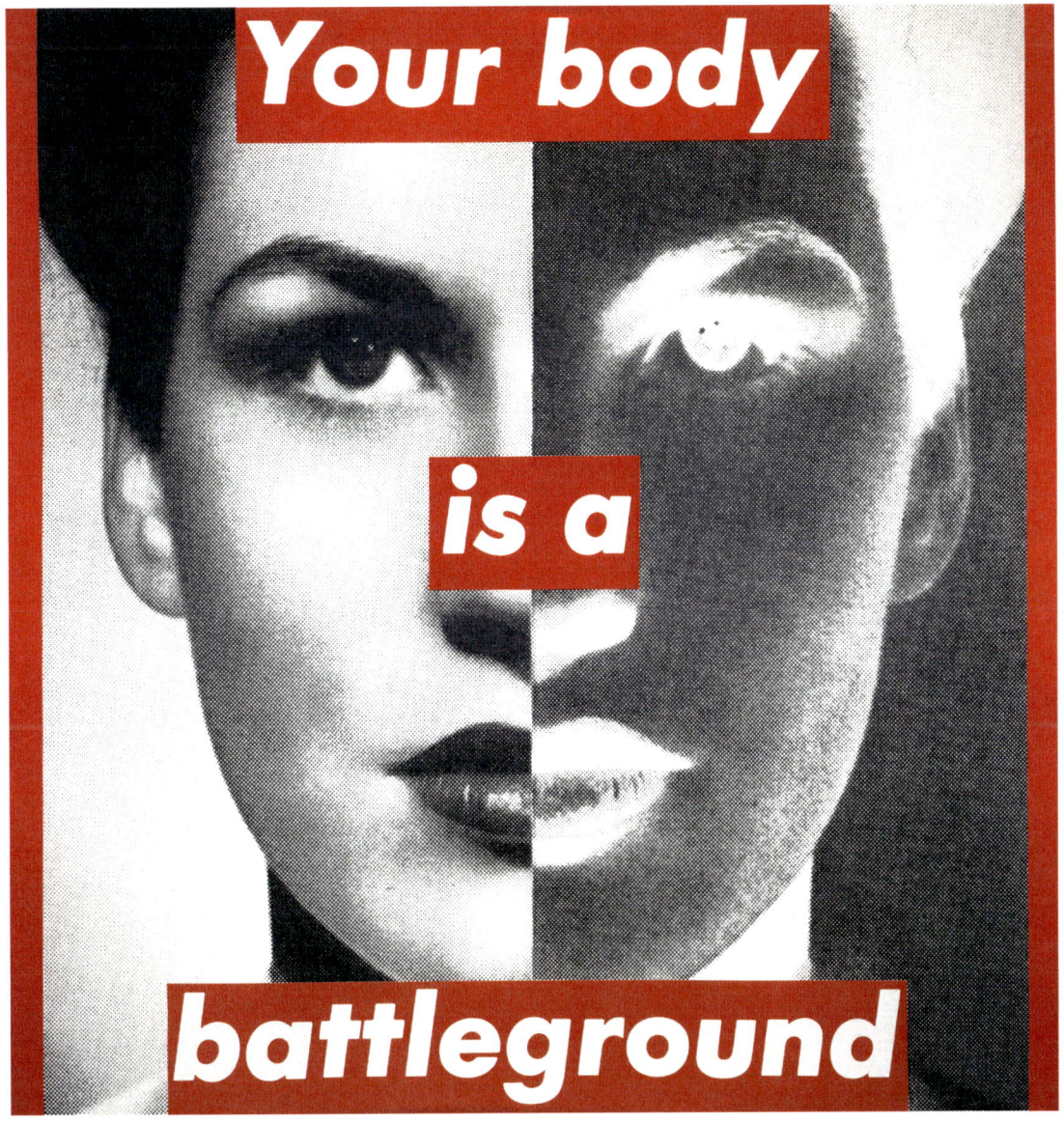

"WHAT WOULD YOU DO IF YOU WEREN'T AFRAID?"[4] asks a poster in Facebook's company office. Corrective legislation and women's rights are important, but the glass ceiling will cease imposing its barriers and will dissipate only when more and more women dare to break through the "glass screens" with which they surround themselves, and do not allow either glass—screen or ceiling—to separate them from the world around them.

In Short

- The glass ceiling obstructs the path of many women seeking self-realization.
- Female artists cracked the glass ceiling by virtue of their breakthrough vision.
- Women "imprison" themselves behind glass partitions.
- Leading female artists broke through:
    » Disconnecting from female stereotypes like Cindy Sherman.
    » Centering on the "self" like Frida Kahlo.
    » Boldness like Georgia O'Keeffe.
    » Determination and assertiveness like Judy Chicago and Barbara Kruger.

Chapter 6

THE FIRST BRUSHSTROKE: STEPPING INTO THE MANAGERIAL ROLE

I decided to start anew, to strip away what I had been taught.
Georgia O'Keeffe

Entering a new role arouses both excitement and apprehension. Much like the artist, the manager entering a new role stands before an empty canvas. For the artist, facing the empty canvas begins with contemplation and thought as to how to incorporate a unique personal statement. It requires planning and preparation. Although in this process, some is unknown and the end result might deviate from the original plan, it begins with a vision of the composition, the color scheme, and the subject matter.

For the manager, the empty canvas is an opportunity and a challenge—to draw a unique professional and personal voice. In the book *Built to Last*: Successful Habits of Visionary Companies, the coauthors James Collins and Jerry Porras claim that a business company with a vision is much like the stupendous paintings by Michelangelo portraying scenes from the Creation narrative on the Sistine Chapel ceiling in the Vatican. The authors note that no single component can be pointed to that causes everything to fall into place and work well, but all the parts integrate into a comprehensive outcome, which is both excellent and sustainable.[1]

"If someone can't climb out of the details and see the bigger picture from multiple angles they're often wrong most of the time," says Jeff Bezos, founder and CEO of

Amazon.[2] The leader must be able to identify business trends and patterns, but equally important is knowing how to combine them into a whole harmonious organizational picture. The new manager who wishes to assert his or her leadership needs to identify principles, set guidelines, and formulate the perception of the role. It is the time to define priorities, focus on challenges and targets. When the message rising from that canvas is authentic, clear, and intentional, the artist-leader can rouse the employees or viewers to feel and to act.

Planning According to Picasso's *Guernica*

The majority of leaders can talk a good vision or strategy, but great leaders are the ones who get things done. Implementing strategy begins with the ability to effectively plan and organize resources and build teamwork. The value of planning cannot be overstated. Researching and putting ideas on paper can be the road map for success.

In 1937, Pablo Picasso completed one of his most outstanding works, **Guernica**. The work documents the destruction and massacre following the bombing of the Spanish village in the Basque named Guernica. Guernica is a huge mural (11.5 ft. in by 25.6 ft.), painted in matte house paint, black-and-white shades only. Long before Picasso revealed this monumental work, he was a well-known and successful artist. Nonetheless, he produced more than 60 preparatory paintings and some eight hundred sketches in a range of styles and compositions. Among them were quickly dashed-off pencil works of the smaller details, as well as paintings that actually look complete. For Picasso, compromise was never part of the equation. He explored and learned every detail that would be in the final work and processed the vision into effective messages. It is hardly a wonder that Guernica is considered one of the greatest works of modern art.

Picasso is just one example of a tradition hundreds of years old in which artists explored and learned their subject by practicing with thoroughness and care before putting down the first layer of color on the empty canvas. That encounter with the blank space is one of the most challenging moments for both the artist and the manager. Like Picasso, a leader must start with a hefty portfolio of sketches outlining the company's future before setting down that first brushstroke.

Planning is one of the foundations of management. Filling that new chair requires advanced planning, forethought, and a detailed outline of what needs to be tackled. But, taking action without planning is almost certainly destined to produce failure. Most likely, managers in a new role carry professional experience, along with individualistic management approaches and perceptions. Previous management experience may make entering the role smoother, but may not prevent some bumpy spots while adapting to the new framework and system. The approach and management style that led a previous organization to success may not necessarily be suited to the current role.

Smart planning begins with learning, listening and observing before setting a strategy, defining goals, and translating those into action. Planning the new role must take into consideration the existing organizational culture's diverse dimensions: symbols and codes of conduct of the organization's members, guiding values, outlooks, and management and activity regulations. The new manager must integrate those into the goals, values, and processes that will address the organization's challenges in the future.

The Effectiveness of Focus: Caravaggio

Focusing on goals is one of the first and most important lessons taught at the prestigious Harvard University Business School. It is a management focus that helps preserve the framework not so much when a company is flourishing, but when the company experiences periods of uncertainty or must make tough decisions. Steps such as financing new projects, manager participation in meetings, or authorizing business travel, become simpler when they are measured according to their relevance to goals the company wishes to achieve.[3]

Image 14: Michelangelo Caravaggio, *The Denial of Saint Peter*, 1610

Focus can also describe the work of the seventeenth century Italian artist Caravaggio (Michelangelo Caravaggio). He was the first artist to use an external light source to direct the viewer to a focus point in the painting. In his work **The Denial of Saint Peter** (image 14), Caravaggio casts a dramatic beam of light on the subject. Darkness fills the surrounding area to imbue the partially lit figure with dramatic tension and, as can be seen clearly from the painting, this focus further reinforces the message he seeks to convey.

Leaders in the business world understand the importance of focus when seeking business growth. At one particular managers' conference,[4] Jeff Weiner and John Donahoe were interviewed. Weiner, CEO of LinkedIn, is proud of more than 500 million users in two hundred countries worldwide and a growth rate of two new users every second. One of the lessons he learned from Steve Jobs was to ask himself, "If I could do only one thing, what would I choose to do?" It is a question that focuses management on the truly important goals. In general, Weiner's management style emphasizes focusing on a select number of goals and implementing them with excellence. John Donahoe, the former CEO of the huge online commercial center eBay, echoed Weiner's statements and added that the organization he heads sold the communications company Skype, despite it being an excellent company, "because we at eBay understood that we need to focus on electronic commerce, which is the company's business core." As business leaders, both Weiner's and Donahoe's actions reflect those of Caravaggio in marking out their goals and targets. They know that the more focused they are on them, the clearer the message becomes.

Benchmarking: Olympia Impacted by Venus of Urbino

It is reasonable to presume that another manager previously filled the new management role. Learning from the organization's experience and its other managers can shed further light on the role a new manager will fill.

Art is not produced in a vacuum. Learning from peers and past experience is an ancient tradition in the art world, and many artists began by sketching or working under the influence of other great works. The artists' purpose was to learn from the greats, and be inspired by them.

Édouard Manet's renowned work, **Olympia** (image 16) is inspired and influenced by a work painted some three centuries earlier, **Venus of Urbino** (image 15) by the Venetian master, Titian (Tiziano Vecellio). Manet's interpretation of Titian's work may seem similar to the master's, yet is very different in essence. Manet explores the boundaries of both the subject matter's characterization and technique, and challenges the accepted perceptions of his time. No more a Venus—that mythological goddess painted by Titian—but rather, Manet's work presents Olympia, a flesh and blood woman. Her direct gaze lacks shame and indicates clearly to the viewer that she is very far from being a goddess or saint. Manet's alla prima painting technique is also revolutionary. Visitors ridiculed the pale, flat image of Olympia when the painting went on display; Manet's bold approach was considered scandalous even at the Paris Salon des Refuses (an exhibition of artworks rejected by the jury of the official Salon, a major art exhibition in Paris in 1863). This fresh interpretation, as with so many others of his works (this painting, too), positioned Manet as one of the founders of the modern art movement.

Image 15: Titian, *Venus of Urbino*, 1538

Image 16: Édouard Manet, *Olympia*, 1863

When stepping into the new managerial role, the specific knowledge and experience the organization has accrued, as well as the data available on competitors, is of great value in setting an optimal learning curve that helps pinpoint areas for improvement, change, or elimination. In 1983, Kaiser Associates developed a model for teaching effectiveness based on comparisons with competitors, known as benchmarking. The model contains seven measurable quantifiable stages for driving processes and outcomes. Initially the activity, which the company seeks to improve, is identified, the desirable outcome indices are set, and companies suitable for benchmarking are identified. The benchmark must be made relative to a company with similar content, or as is known at Kaiser, "comparing apples to apples." Once the appropriate parameters for comparison have been found, a strategy is consolidated for implementing the comparison while controlling the indices and outcomes defined at the start of the process.

It is natural, upon entering a new managerial role, to want to leave one's mark on the organization. Sam Walton, founder of the Walmart chain, said innumerable times that it was competitors who drove his success. "Almost everything I've done, I learned from someone else. More than anyone else, I visited many headquarter offices of cheap outlet chains. I asked questions about pricing policy and distribution methods. That's how I learned a lot." Walton became a model for his employees of a person who never ceases to learn from competitors, even from "the worst" competitors. According to Walton, even they have something worth emulating.[5]

Biographical books on successful managers show how experience and knowledge are their most important tools. Management books are collections of organizational and managerial success stories—like former General Electric CEO Jack Welch's autobiography, Jack: Straight from the Gut. Books like The Seven Habits of Highly Effective People by Stephen Covey or Built to Last by James Collins and Jerry

Porras are must-haves for every manager. They inspire, and point new managers toward the tools for managerial success.

Clean, empty, the canvas holds inherent and rare opportunities, and great promise coupled with challenge. That first brushstroke may have an inordinate effect on what comes next, and even determine the artwork's future. Will the leader successfully embed her or his personal mark? These and other related questions are just some of the dilemmas encountered by every artist, manager, or leader. Jeff Weiner, CEO of LinkedIn, and John Donahoe, CEO of eBay, emphasized the importance of focusing on goals, while Sam Walton points to the contribution of benchmarking in an organization's success. Goal focusing and benchmarking can turn an existing work into a new work, and make managers taking on a new role into impactful leaders leaving as unique a statement as that of former leaders.

In Short

- The empty canvas is an opportunity and a challenge for both artists and leaders.
- Vision can be formulated and shaped by the empty canvas.
- Like artists, before tackling the empty canvas with the first actions:
    - » Plan like Picasso in creating a masterpiece like Guernica.
    - » Focus on main goals to convey a strong message like Caravaggio.
    - » Learn from peers as a source of inspiration as seen in Manet's Olympia.

PART III
MOTIVATION

Chapter 7

LEADING CHANGE LIKE PABLO PICASSO

Most leaders talk about change, but most are just managing momentum.
                                                                Jeff Immelt

Change is the most constant aspect of life and business in our times. Immense disruption driven by connectivity and new technologies are redefining business strategy. The challenge to leadership is to shake up the status quo, to encourage reforms, and pave the way for opportunities. The late Warren Bennis, a renowned expert on management and organizational behavior, saw the leader as the person who renews, develops, and leads the breakthrough during a crisis. By contrast, John Kotter, a professor of leadership, sees the manager as the person who challenges the status quo, brings innovation and reforms, and paves new avenues by setting new goals. Despite the differences between the two approaches, they share a common denominator: both drive change. In the words of Marissa Mayer, CEO of Yahoo, it is a choice to "change, or be changed."[1] Leaders can easily rest on their laurels and enjoy the fruits of the current business model and forget that their role is to continue to reinvent the organization. In a Harvard Business Review article titled "The CEO's Role in Business Model Reinvention", the authors recommend that managers ensure the organization is operating at three levels:

- Managing current situations through data analysis, indices, and outcomes, and creating organizational harmony

- Selective forgetting of the past while mapping future trends
- Creating the future by integrating additional nontraditional "voices" when shaping organizational harmony.[2]

Pablo Picasso's incredible artistic career can be a colorful source of inspiration for the business world. Picasso was an innovator and a change-maker and is probably considered the most important artist of the twentieth century. A predominant characteristic was his drive for stylistic change throughout his long creative life. His works, in fact, implement those three levels: managing the present through uncompromising professional activity, selective forgetting of the past, and adopting chosen traits from the world of art that preceded him for the sake of creating his future.

Picasso's vast talent was revealed while still young. He began painting at seven years old. While still a teen with no formal art training, his virtuosity became apparent in realistic works that bettered those of his teacher, his very own father, who himself was a renowned artist. From this period, more than two thousand paintings have been preserved. He was already in his prime as an artist even before beginning his professional artistic career; but that did not satisfy him. If he was able to paint his mother with such precision (image 17), why did he choose, a decade later, to paint his own self-portrait in a primitive style (image 18) recalling ethnic African masks?

The difference between the two portraits is a function of Picasso's professional path, where he refused to settle for current or past successes. Picasso's greatness derives from constant seeking. He created new directions, and in his work gave artistic expression to both the internal and external changes, which included personal events on one hand, and dialogue with the fields of literature, philosophy, and science on the other. Picasso never rested for a moment in this act of seeking,

Image 17: Pablo Picasso, *The Artist's Mother*, 1896
© succession Picasso 2017

Image 18: Pablo Picasso, *Self-portrait*, 1907
© succession Picasso 2017

and broke through his own boundaries repeatedly, developing new artistic styles and languages. He was a pioneer leading to change that impacted the culture of the twentieth century, and our perceptions of art.

Trial and Experimentation: "If I Don't Look, I Won't Find."

Picasso's earliest works already show his interest in testing the waters and inventiveness. He stated that as a child, he spent four years studying to paint like Raphael, but then needed 50 years to return to painting like a child. His ideas and style did not come about in a vacuum but were based on earlier knowledge. Initially, his professional path in driving stylistic change was one of observing the works of renowned artists, but instead of precisely emulating them, as is common in art study programs, Picasso created new connections to them in a process of trial and investigation, adopting and melding several stylistic influences in one work. For example, in his painting **Margot** from 1897, he merges a mix of styles influenced by artists of his generation: Georges Seurat (Pointillism), Vincent van Gogh (Post-Impressionism), Paul Gaugin (Symbolism), and Henri Matisse (Fauvism). Picasso seemed to be entertaining himself, without knowing quite where the outcome would lead, but these efforts quickly showed their value in helping him test, explore, and consolidate a new language of his own making.

The significance of "If I don't look, I won't find" is vital to people in the business world in this time of enormous disruption. Success in business is defined to a great degree by the ability to turn ideas into value faster than the competition. The capacity to turn ideas into a new product is faster today than ever before. It is the role of the leadership to promote a culture that will embrace innovation and change. Like Picasso, leaders need to boldly encourage curiosity, risk-taking, playfulness, and experimentation.

External Change: Einstein and the Dimension of Time

Image 19: Pablo Picasso, *Violin*, 1912 © succession Picasso 2017

From 1905 on, Picasso concentrated primarily on attempting to react to diverse influences in his environment. His artistic leadership and intellectual curiosity attracted him to innovative theories of his time from the fields of physics, philosophy, music, and theater. The theory of relativity published in 1905, as proposed by Albert Einstein, had a strong impact on Picasso. One of the conclusions Einstein reached was that two events simultaneously occurring in two different spaces depend on the movement of their viewers.

Einstein's studies of time and space aroused Picasso's curiosity, and led him into exploring the concept of space and time on a flat canvas. In 1907, he embarked on a new language and painted his first Cubist work, **Les Demoiselles d'Avignon**. In his Cubist works, such as **Violin** (image 19), Picasso breaks the violin down into geometric planes and fans them out. In this way, he enables the viewer to see all its parts at once. The flat objects become new entities seen simultaneously from all angles. In the same way as he did at the start of his career, merging different styles together into one piece, Picasso here, too, integrates innovative theories from external sources such as science and culture into his art.

The impact of external changes on organizations is particularly powerful today. The relentless march of innovation has forced some of the world's major technology companies to take painful measures. In late 2016, Cisco Systems had not identified the shift from in-house, online networks to remote data centers and that led to the layoffs of 14,000 employees, roughly 20 percent of its workforce. Intel also failed to identify the weakening laptop market in time, and the result was layoffs of 11,000 employees by 2016. Intel's Chairperson, Andy Bryant, stated that the company had "lost its way."

Organizations must develop a proactive mechanism (seismograph) to monitor and react to external influences such as those seen with Intel and Cisco. Changes in government, resources, customer needs, competition, or technology impact organizations. Analysis and ongoing scanning of these external forces of change can be done with managerial tools such as SWOT (Strengths, Weakness, Opportunities, Threats) or PEST (Political, Economic, Social, Technological) to identify strategic steps to adopt. Like Picasso, external changes can be viewed as opportunities to embark toward a new frontier of creativity.

Internal Changes: The Blue, Pink and Black Periods

Picasso's curiosity and drive to experiment and develop a unique artistic identity led him to continued movement between styles. Events in his personal life affected him internally, seeping into his artwork. Thus, for example, the 1901 suicide of his best friend, Carlos Casagemas, left its emotional imprint: Picasso began painting primarily in shades of blue. This stylistic change, during which he created hundreds of paintings such as the work titled La Vie, based on leaden blues, became known as "the blue period."

New love in 1904 with the young model Fernande Olivier ended the three-year blue period and opened "the pink period." Once again, Picasso devoted himself to personal experiences and allowed them to impact his work; pink expresses his changed mood throughout another three-year period. His exposure to Iberian and African masks and figurines highly popular in Paris at the time brought on a third, specific period, "the black period," which paved the way toward his first Cubist works. Together, the blue, pink, and black periods reflected monochromatic harmonies that were innovative and individualistic, and were breakthroughs.

In the business world, internal environmental factors such as organizational structure, people, culture, and leadership style affect business outcome. Driving internal change in organizations is an ongoing challenge. Courage and vision are needed to lead internal changes in a company so that it matches the external environmental challenges. An example of such change can be seen in the online merchant, eBay. In 2004, the company's stock peaked, but from 2007 on it began to weaken. In 2009, it had already lost some 80 percent of its peak value. Appointing John Donahoe as CEO led to an amazing turnaround, with revenue growing 23 percent. One of the unpopular moves the new CEO made was to replace the company's entire senior management. In Donahoe's view, a dramatic change in the company's leadership was vital to attaining the next level. One of the toughest challenges facing a large company is recruiting the best people—disruptive changers who penetrate and drive change. Donahoe's new management team was a partner to his approach, the goal of which was to lead the structuring of a wonderful stable company over the long term.[3]

Courage and Professionalism: From Realism to Surrealism

Picasso's leadership in the field of modern art can serve as a role model for the business world at both the personal and organizational levels. From him we can learn about leading change through dynamic, developing vision. Picasso never rested on his laurels. His virtuosity drove him to push the boundaries further and further. He was one of the first to test the idea of using newspaper scraps, thereby inventing collage (Synthetic Cubism). He inserted letters into his painting. Influenced by Surrealism, he warped his painting's figures. Even though his childhood aspiration as a painter was based on naïveté and spontaneity, throughout his life he preserved the levels of his academic training. Each of his works was first explored deeply through multiple sketches and preparatory drafts in pencil and paint.

In **Portrait of Sylvette 1** (image 20) and **Sylvette David in a Green Armchair** (image 21), the various stages of the process are exposed, with Picasso analyzing the object as a means of bringing it to express his unique language. He begins with the realistic sketch (image 4) and abstracts it until it's his own unique language (image 5). These works are great examples of his way of thinking and mode of working. The change he drove was always the outcome of careful forethought and highly developed skill, merged with courage and vision, or as he himself put it, "I paint objects as I think them, not as I see them."

At the World Economic Forum in Davos[4], Switzerland, a discussion delved into leadership in a world of risks. Orit Gadiesh, Chair of Bain & Company, an international consultancy, was one of the speakers. She noted that too many leaders avoid driving change, claiming that the risk was too high, but in fact the risk of stagnation is even greater and comes from a lack of understanding and knowledge.

Image 21: Pablo Picasso, *Sylvette David in a Green Armchair*, 1954 © succession Picasso 2017

Image 20: Pablo Picasso, *Portrait of Sylvette 1*, 1954 © succession Picasso 2017

In that same discussion, John Chambers, President and Chair of Cisco, noted that many of Cisco's competitors have disappeared from the business world map over the past two decades. If Cisco had not taken courageous, self-renewing steps that involved risk it, too, would have been long since left behind.

Frequent shifts from an "old" to a "new" style involve forgoing the sense of inherent security offered by staying in a "comfort zone" for the sake of a foray into unexplored territory. Too many managers, however, are not quick to accept the need for change. They are comfortable in their familiar business environment where they are assured control over what already exists, believing that time will prove their decisions to be right. But business organizations guided by this kind of thinking tend to postpone decisive choices, resulting in change occurring under crisis conditions. In this way, organizations fall into the "excellence trap" that fixes them into a known, familiar slot. Picasso did not succumb to merely showing achievement and excellence in familiar work methods. Rather, these two traits led him to courageous experimentation in creating new things. Had he not aspired to breaking through and beyond the familiar, Picasso may never have earned admiration in history as one of the twentieth century's greatest cultural leaders and artists. It was his ability to proactively initiate change and take the risk of leaving his comfort zone that opened up avenues of success.

The same thoroughness employed by Picasso when exploring stylistic change should be the guideline for the manager-leader when considering the consequences of change before it is implemented. Like Picasso, while moving from the "old" to the "new", it is important to rely on the mastery of previous know-how. Change leadership should "honor history" and depart from it.[5] Opposition to change on the part of stakeholders is one of the greatest obstacles. Coca Cola's alteration, some years ago, to its secret recipe led to sweeping opposition by consumers worldwide, forcing the company to withdraw from its plans. Another example relates to Netflix, the American company that provides movie rentals to subscribers. At the end of 2011, the company announced a change in its pricing structure. Overnight, it lost one million clients.

Opposition to change is a common reaction, deriving from a range of factors, which include habit, conservatism, mistrust of management, and fear of economic or status losses. Various studies have shown that more than half the processes of change in organizations are doomed to failure due to insufficient advance preparation. Before driving change, the organization's leadership must understand the organization's most basic mechanisms, develop clear programs, analyze the forces influencing its environment, and take steps to overcome anticipated opposition as it aims to garner the commitment of all stakeholders.

"Everything you can imagine is real," Picasso said. Indeed, leadership that operates out of commitment to an innovative dynamic vision and manages changes skillfully and professionally can turn the innovative vision into reality.

In Short

- "Change or be changed," in Marissa Mayer's words.
- "The success trap" is an obstacle to identify, realize, and lead change.
- Picasso's motto "I don't look, I find" made him the cultural leader he is.
- Change can be inspired from both external and internal variables.
- The courage to drive change begins with vision, but requires in-depth research and advance preparation.
- Minimizing resistance to change requires skillful planning.

Chapter 8

THE FOUNTAIN OF INNOVATION

Art does not reproduce the visible; rather, it makes visible.
Paul Klee

In the 1960s, the average life span of major corporations in the S&P Index was about 60 years, while in 2016 the average time is less than 20 years. In this business environment, there are greater pressures on corporations to (out) perform, to reach greater levels of financial return. Organizations need not only adapt to changes but also focus on opportunities and growth. Major companies not adapting to the current technology landscape or rapid changes within their sector, such as Kodak or Blockbuster, have either gone under or lost their relevance. It should come as no surprise that innovation is a major key to dealing with these challenges. For organizations to become the spearheads in their field, innovation should be a part of the organization's DNA.[1]

In the modern art world, innovation is a necessity. The relevance of the modern artist is measured to a great degree by their ability to refresh aesthetic concepts. Artists observe and question their environment while fulfilling a constant drive to create beauty and meaning. Many artists who are now seen as cultural leaders created a new future, starting with Leonardo da Vinci, a sixteenth-century innovator, and artists of our own time like Damien Hirst or Ai Weiwei. These artists often work in a state of existential and professional uncertainty, but nonetheless have the courage to take risks and develop new artistic languages even if rejected by their contemporaries.

Innovation is about converting imagination and vision into thought, and thought into ideas and action. Innovation involves experimentation and risk-taking; mental and physical boundaries need to be overcome. Great innovative ideas are a result of a process, but they do not necessarily reveal themselves through structured processes and cannot be forced to come into existence. Often they simply seem to surface; in other instances, they begin as images arising from an existing idea. Reaching them cannot always come from the shortest, fastest path since the road is often unknown. The link between art and innovative business is the catalyst that not only leads to a type of ex nihilo, but also to ex aliquo (something from something) creation in the sense of examining what is for the sake of what might be.

Innovation also involves failure, but lack of innovation leads to stagnancy. Elon Musk is the legendary entrepreneur and founder of PayPal, Tesla Motors, Solar City, and Space X. In early 2016, overcoming competition, NASA awarded Space X a Commercial Orbital Transportation Services (COTS) agreement. The success of Space X is not surprising because Musk, who is known for saying "Failure is an option here. If things are not failing, you are not innovating enough," is a great visionary and a risk-taker. In September 2016, the rocket Falcon 9 that was launched by Space X exploded in the air. Musk tweeted immediately after: "Turning out to be the most difficult and complex failure we have over 14 years." Failure can be costly, but failure is also a catalyst for growth.

A Culture of Innovation

Internet giants, the technology companies such as Microsoft, Yahoo, Google, and Amazon have been leaders since the beginning of the 2000s on the ComScore Scale, the global media measurement and analytics company. These organizations preserve their top listings with very little shifting of position, their stability being a function of the huge resources that would be needed to topple them. The risk of being toppled does not depend so much on innovation by competitors but on stagnation or fixation at the organizational level. Bill Gates, Microsoft CEO, describes how the company's culture is typified by an approach in which "I see us as an underdog today, just as I've seen us as an underdog every day for the last 20 years. If we don't maintain that perspective, some competitor will eat our lunch."[2]

Gates's attitude shows the great importance of leadership in building and nurturing an organizational culture that encourages innovation, curiosity, observation, asking the questions, self-expression, courage, and the passion to experiment. In a study conducted in 2013 by the international consultancy Booz & Company, with the California Silicon Valley regional economic board, 1,000 public global companies and 275 Silicon Valley companies were examined. The research found that 46 percent of the local companies operated on the basis of an innovation strategy, and only 19 percent of global companies operated with the same approach. The organizational culture of Silicon Valley companies was in fact the "secret ingredient" that assisted them in being the technology world's spearheads.[3]

An innovation-focused organizational culture is born of the commitment by the person who tops the pyramid. But this kind of culture shouldn't be the sole domain of the R&D department: it should also be integral to the activities of all employees in an organization. In *Extreme Management*, Mark Stevens writes, "The individual is the fountainhead of creativity and innovation… Only by releasing the energy and fire of our employees can we achieve the decisive, continuous productivity advantages…"[4] Innovation is the solution to challenges, and leadership advances mechanisms that allow for creative thinking, which leads to these solutions. This kind of leadership builds on encouraging experimentation, initiative, and risk-taking, and tolerating failed attempts with patience.

Innovation: Outcome of Inspiration, or Spark of Genius?

Purposeful and methodical innovation begins with analyzing sources for new business opportunities, claimed Peter Drucker. Innovative people go out into the field, look around, ask questions, and listen attentively. Analyzing the probability of a business opportunity means right and left brain activity.[5] Sophie Blum, CEO of Proctor & Gamble Israel, believes that innovative leaders are not born so much as become that way, and that innovation should be a part of every employee's responsibility. The ability to feel comfortable with uncertainty is an art, as is the ability to keep an open mind, cooperate with consumers, and be ready to receive breakthrough ideas from diverse fields and branches. It is an acquired art that can be methodically taught in a society and nurtured by enthusiasm.[6]

Art identifies two main axes of innovation: experimental and conceptual. Experimental innovation involves searching for and studying a goal in a measured, consistent manner and learning is prioritized over the finished product. Experimental artists are generally those who do not prepare drafts and early sketches. Their professional experience builds gradually, and the innovative element of their work appears in stages. Conceptual innovation in art occurs from within carefully planned and defined goal focusing aimed at expressing an idea or emotion. Conceptual innovators learn their topic well through advance preparation. Synthesizing existing ideas and techniques serves to achieve the goal in a methodical manner,[7] but in fact, innovation is usually the end result of conscious, directed seeking for the opportunity to renew. The act of seeking is real work and should be carried out as though the seeker is indeed an artist.[8]

Coloring the Familiar Box with a New Shade: Henri Matisse

With Matisse, for the first time, color did not serve as a mirror of objectivity, but expressed release from norms and an independent essentiality. **Woman with a Hat** (image 22) is definitely a portrait as far as criteria relating to its similarity to the painted model, other than its coloration, which tells a new story. Matisse colors the woman's face in yellow, green, pink and blue. He deviates from the traditional descriptions of external reality in preference for manifesting their internal, subjective reality.

To a viewer of our current period this is hardly innovative, but at the start of the twentieth century it was a true revolution.

In the business world, the battle for the consumer's heart and pocket is an ongoing challenge. Apple pioneered and developed the iPhone, a smartphone with a touch screen and apps. Competitors did not offer the market original ideas and a different smartphone, but produced phones that fed off the iPhone's characteristics and look. Currently, the mobile phone war is primarily between Apple and Samsung but both use the same "colors" for their "boxes." New competitors in the smartphone industry are breathing hard down both these companies' necks, competing

Image 22: Henri Matisse, *Woman with a Hat*, 1905

with them by offering similar "boxes" with a significantly lower price.

But to lead in a sated market, smartphones must be colored in bright new hues translated into smart technological solutions and content, such as the Apple Watch or Google Glass that might replace the familiar smartphone in the future. Just as Matisse "rewired" color into a familiar template—that of the portrait—and thereby shaped a new language, so business organizations must keep seeking "the next great thing," those products that bear new tidings and are not mimics or copies of existing products but the outcome of thought that colors the familiar in new hues.

How Simple to Simplify: Piet Mondrian

Abstract art does not usually present a topic or image of a recognizable body but rather, expresses emotions or ideas through artistic means such as color, texture, and composition. The central concept in Piet Mondrian's work, **Composition** (image 23) is that the painting is structured on the fundamental elements of line and color in order to abstract characteristics and refine the essence into a clean, primeval "language of art."

The term "reverse innovation," coined by two Dartmouth professors—Vijay Govindarajan and Chris Trimble—and subsequently popularized by GE's Jeffrey R. Immelt, refers to products used first in the developing world. In the process of reverse innovation, products are "watered-down" to basic functionality for sale in poorer countries, and then moved upstream back to the developed world. Most tech products tend to be feature-intensive to reflect the abilities of the company behind the product while also addressing a constantly expanding circle of technology users who thrive on multiple smart functions. However, there is also a large stratum of consumers who do not enjoy this abundance, and do not need so many features. They want very little more than the on and off buttons. In the same way that top fashion designers produce unique models for their prestigious shows, and "simplified" models for clients seeking some prestige combined with functionality, it is possible to create an alternative product with uncompromising quality but simpler functionality.

Image 23: Piet Mondrian, *Composition*, 1923

Dr. Genevieve Bell, director of the Intel International research department, described in a September 2011 interview with CNN how the company altered products to suit consumer needs. Intel's state of the art processors offer too many functions for clients in many parts of the developing world compared to the needs of consumers in the developed world, which usually wants super-speed processors. In the emerging markets, the Internet is primarily used for sending text messages; in such countries, cheap, simplified processors address market needs. Distinguishing the characteristics of the two types of consumers is a dynamic concept. Over time, and as globalization spreads, the developing world will also move higher up the ladder of progress. Should a consumer market shift occur in those countries, successful organizations would be the ones that identify and reflect the shift toward greater cutting edge demand by adapting their products accordingly.

Examining Under a Different Light: Claude Monet and the Impressionists

Managers and organizations tend to see products or services under a single spotlight: the purpose for which those products were created. Casting light, both actual and metaphorical, from different angles to examine the organization or product can bring about insights and lead to actions. The clearest example of this can be seen in the artwork of Claude Monet who, as noted, sought to document the subject of his work under varying conditions. He painted each subject repeatedly, each time trying to catch the influence of light on the subject at different hours of the day. Series such as Rouen Cathedral, Water Lilies, Hay Stacks, St. Lazare Train Station and many more are offered in multiple versions. Monet studied how light affects our sight in the way a scientist works in the laboratory, methodically and with focus. The subjects chosen for his various series were identical, but the light at the time of painting creates a unique narrative for each work.

In the business world, too, existing products can be cast in new light. The printer is one excellent example. Printing on paper is par for the course in modern life, but recently the home printer was recast in new light, with the development of the 3-D printer functioning in much the same way as familiar ink printers. Instead of spraying ink on paper, these "printers" spray layer upon superfine layer of polymer or metal, which hardens during the printing process. In this way, objects can be made from almost any materials. The 3-D printing is revolutionizing and improving quality of life and productivity. It is now possible to print on-demand a building or even a human body part, like a torso. Its influence is already seen in many fields such as aerospace, medical, dental, jewelry, architecture, and automotive. Based on data from the Global Industry Analysts Company, the market value for 3-D printers is expected to reach about $19 billion by 2020.

Disassemble, Flatten, Reassemble: Picasso

Cubism, the avant-garde art style that led to an artistic revolution in the early twentieth century, sees the painted objects from all angles simultaneously. For example, Picasso's portrait of the art dealer Henry Kahnweiler or **Violin** (image 19) by are spread across the canvas like a fanned pack of cards as if it was reengineered. In the business world, reengineering, a management theory developed by Dr. Michael Hammer of Columbia University, focuses on creating fundamental change in an organization by reshaping it after rethinking its structure, processes, roles, and decision-making. Emphasis should be placed on creative, revolutionary thinking. In late 2014, Hewlett Packard announced plans to split the PC and printer business from its enterprise products and service business. It resulted in two companies: HP Inc. and Hewlett Packard Enterprise. In doing so, Meg Whitman, the CEO, implemented her vision to disassemble the giant company and to reassemble as two smaller, focused, and agile companies. The reengineering of HP as well as Picasso's Cubism disassembles the subject into its parts, to open new opportunities for restructuring a new, innovative business image.

Developing New Uses: Marcel Duchamp and the "Ready Made"

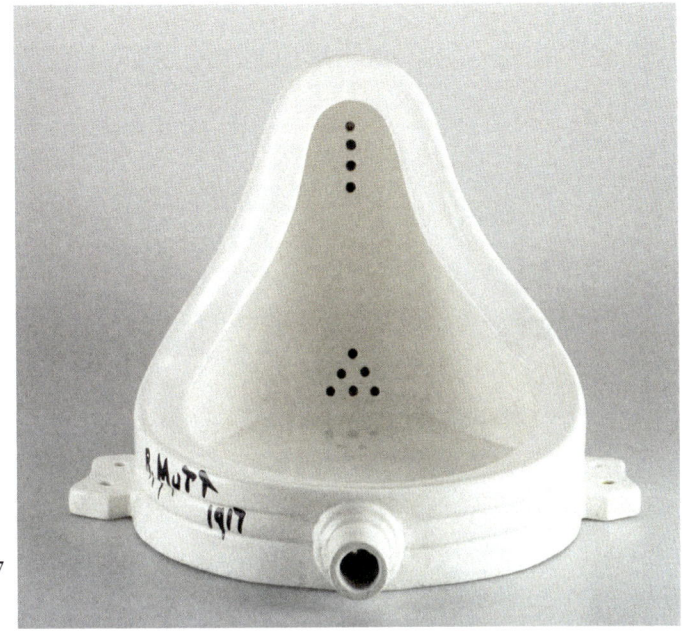

Image 24: Marcel Duchamp, *Fountain*, 1917

In 1917, the artist Marcel Duchamp presented a urinal in the Society of Independent Artists Exhibition at Grand Central Gallery, New York, and signed the manufacturer's name: "R. Mutt, 1917." This work, which he titled **Fountain** (image 24) fanned a storm and led to rousing in-depth discussion on the question, "What is art?" Duchamp redesignated a ready-made object as art.

Re-designation of a product in the business world can lead to a conceptual or physical breakthrough. Sometimes, the next product in an organization is pretty much on the company's shelf, but stagnant thinking inhibits its development—remember what happened to Kodak. Toward the end of the nineteenth century, scientists began studying the nature of botulin toxin because of its beneficial effects on neuromuscular disease, which usually appeared after eating contaminated food, and was called "botulism" at the time. Botulism was even known to cause death when paralyzed muscles caused respiratory failure. Since then, botulin has been used to treat many other pathologies, but what gave this toxin instant star status was when dermatologists and surgeons in the field of cosmetics began using it, taking advantage of its ability to paralyze muscles and make wrinkles disappear. The rise of sales in Botox is dizzying; when initial reports of its cosmetic use began surfacing in 1993, the scope of global sales shot to $25 million per annum. In 2002, that figure had reached $430 million, in 2009 was at $1.3 billion, and in 2015 it jumped to $4.2 billion.

Repackaging: Christo

Product packaging holds an important function in our current competitive business world. Steve Jobs was known for his high level of involvement in all stages of product development and design at Apple. He repeatedly sent the new iPhone back to his planners and designers until they reached what he perceived as the perfect

Image 25: Christo, *Wrapped Reichstag*, Germany, 1995

packaging. Jobs understood that the user experience begins with packaging, which narrates the product's story.

Christo, the environmental artist, began repackaging objects in 1958 by wrapping them in cloth. Shortly after shortening his name from its full Christo Vladimirov Javashev, he joined forces with Jeanne-Claude de Guillebon and together they wrapped public buildings and select spaces in nature, creating a kind of "new packaging." In Christo's view, the cloth revealed the object's outline but hid its details, making it softer and more sensual. Wrapping allowed redefining the object's domain or territory and seeing the whole with a holistic view that aided observation of the object's essence. Indeed, Christo wrapped trees, Florida Key islands, Central Park in New York, and civic buildings like the Reichstag (image 25).

In the world of marketing, wrapping and packaging is an inseparable part of the total product. As with Christo's wraps, the packaging creates a dialogue with the product and empowers its existence.

Increase or Decrease: Alberto Giacometti

Size is another dominant trait used by artists to portray familiar images in a newly conceived language. It can seen clearly in the works of the Swiss sculptor Alberto Giacometti. Exaggerated dimensions and unique shapes that reflect the isolation of humans in the modern era characterize his bronze statues, with their skinny and lengthened limbs. Giacometti's conceptual differentiation, as manifested by the sizing of common objects, undoubtedly played a part in bringing his work to the public's attention and leading to his success.

In business, too, size counts and can differentiate a product. McDonalds was among the pioneers to realize market potential of "Super-size" meals. In the smartphones arena, after Nokia lost its leading status in the market, it attempted to close the gap by differentiating itself from competitors by size. Nokia was among the first cellular companies to introduce the "Phablet," an oversized smartphone to combine the functions of both smartphone with tablet. However, it proved to be too late for the company to regain its dominance because when it comes to innovation, timing is of the essence.

Attentive to the Zeitgeist: Andy Warhol

Uberization is coined after the great success of Uber Technologies, the company that provides taxi rides in a new business model. Uber was there just in time, alert to the spirit of the times when technology and social media were the catalysts to peer-to-peer transactions across industries. Precisely in these times, when change is the name of the game, businesses need to be attentive to current tendencies as a way of minimizing any damage to their organizations and their leading status.

Paying attention to the zeitgeist, a German term meaning roughly "the spirit of the times," was the main source of inspiration for the Pop artists' works, and particularly those of Andy Warhol, who produced primarily in the 1960s. New York and the post-World War II years were fertile ground for Andy Warhol. Economic abundance, mass production, and a developing consumer culture all impacted the artist. Mass marketing of brand names on billboards and colorful neon signs throughout the city fed his artistic vision.

Warhol reacted and captured the spirit of his times and urban environment by using images taken from mass culture and brand admiration (image 26).

In this way, he carved out a place for himself as the most famous and familiar Pop artist of the modern art era. Many of Warhol's artworks show an identical image: methodical, almost exact duplication of a popular item such as a bottle of Coca Cola, or well-known figures such as Elvis Presley, Marilyn Monroe, and even himself in self-portraits. All these works have the feel of an industrialized assembly line. Taking on the industrialized / marketing assembly line, Warhol used materials and techniques employed by industry rather than those of the world of art. His creative works trumpeted the times. His vision, manifested in his artwork, reflects that period.

Image 26: Andy Warhol, *Campbell's Soup*, 1968

The commercialization and mass production that fueled Warhol's artistic vision today fuels the vision of current entrepreneurs. Social media is today's largest "assembly line" and a major enabler of peer-to-peer marketing and the sharing economy. Two young entrepreneurs from San Francisco, Joe Gebbia and Brian Chesky, were among the first to recognize its potential. They cofounded Airbnb, a company providing hosting that began with airbeds and breakfast. Gebbia and Chesky identified the need in October 2007, when a conference held by The Industrial Designers Society of America took place in San Francisco. It was obvious that there were not enough hotel rooms for participants streaming into the city. The two spread inflatable mattresses around their living room and hosted three guests, asking friends to do the same.

By summer of 2013, Airbnb was operating in some 200 countries and 35,000 cities throughout the world, providing solutions especially during peak tourist seasons for some 200,000 guests per day. Very quickly the service offered not only lodgings in the homes of local, private hosts, but expanded to full holiday packages that included anything from airport valet service to being shown around local sightseeing spots. Like Warhol, the vision shared by Gebbia and Chesky as entrepreneurs and leaders reflects and affects the new era where peer-to-peer economy and the social media are the "new assembly line" of ideas, markets, and innovation.

The Rule is That There are No Rules: Postmodernism

In postmodern art there are no rules and regulations, nor any binding theory. There is, however, a multifaceted diversity of ideas that tie materials to unconventional techniques. This challenges perceptions and produces the unexpected. Postmodernism undermines the superiority of the creator and the validity of defined interpretations. The multiplicity of perspectives, outlooks, and cultures is typical of both the observer and the creator.

Postmodern thinking encourages paradox; blurs or merges opposites, contrasts, and boundaries; does not attempt to present an organized narrative; and yet a kind of narrative takes shape, the result of the interaction between the viewer and the artwork. In an exhibition in the art museum of Vienna, the contemporary artist Erwin Wurm presents a house that seems to have fallen from the sky onto the museum's facade. **In House Attack** (image 27), the artist's role is one of mediator. He does not impose any meaning on his work; he only provides an initial aesthetic stimulant. The rest is up to the viewers, who can choose to reveal whatever hidden meanings they wish in this unexpected work.

Our current business climate can be compared to the postmodern era in art. The development of expanding globalization, processes of accelerated privatization, unstable financial markets, and the fast pacing of technology and information transfer impact not only business competition but every sphere of life. What was acceptable yesterday is not necessarily so today, and almost certainly will not be tomorrow. As such, the rules and business norms of the past do not hold for the future. Postmodern thinking does not seek to offer organized solutions, theories, or formulas that enforce uniformity. Postmodern thinking releases the artist from the remains of those stylistic chains from the past and opens up legitimacy to innovative and free expression.

Image 27: Erwin Wurm, *House Attack*, 2006

Constructive Disruptiveness: Disruptive Changers

In the business world, innovation and creativity are measured according to their cost and their degree of effectiveness, but even in a world of constraints, it is still possible to think outside the box. John Donahoe, CEO of eBay, noted on entering his role that he identified the need to upgrade the company's website and develop smartphone applications. He recruited several young talents from outside the company, known as disruptive changers, and was surprised by the results. These young people said they needed to physically distance from the routines of their lives, and asked to be flown to Australia. Even though he was taken aback by their irregular request, he granted it. They set out for "Down Under" and four months later developed the new site and smartphone app, to the satisfaction of the board, and at a cost of only some tens of thousands of dollars. In Donahoe's words, had the project been left in the hands of the company's technology development department, it would likely have taken two years, and ended up costing millions of dollars. In a huge concern such as eBay and others like it, the challenge to drive innovation is huge, making the role of leadership so important to breaking through frozen thought patterns and barriers and challenging the standardized views.[9]

"The best way to predict the future is to create it," said leadership guru Peter Drucker. The future is an unpredictable variable determined by events in the present, which means there can be innumerable scenarios of the future. In encouraging an organizational culture of innovation, the multidimensional perception that postmodernism drives can open current organizations to accessing new concepts and opportunities. Leaders need to empower and challenge people to inquire, to embrace uncertainty, to doubt and to realize their creativity.[10] The conceptual artist

Joseph Beuys said that every human is an artist as long as one keeps curiosity for introspection, endeavor, and exploration. Organizations do not necessarily need to change the criteria of light, packaging, proportions, or abstraction. The guiding principle should be that there are no fixed rules.

In Short

- Modern art speaks in the language of innovation.
- The role of leadership is to direct, drive, and develop a culture of innovation.
- Innovation-geared culture promotes curiosity, experimentation, self-expression, and creativity.
- Innovation can surface from coincidence or from planned conceptual search.
- Like artists, leaders can:
    » Paint the old box with new colors, like Henry Matisse.
    » Examine products or processes under different light, like Claude Monet.
    » Rewrap ideas and products to show their qualities, like Christo.
    » Be attentive to the spirit of the time, like Andy Warhol.
    » Simplify to show the essence, like Piet Mondrian.
    » The rule of innovation is that are no rules, as seen in Erwin Wurm's work.

Chapter 9

COACHING vs. MENTORING: The two "Mona Lisa"

Tell me—and I will not forget. Show me—and I will remember. Let me try—and then I can understand.
                                                                                                                                                    Confucius

Leaders are measured by their achievements. Both talent and effort are required to lead, however; organizational success cannot rely only on the merit of the leader. It should be a collaborative effort shared with colleagues and employees. To realize people potential, leaders need to harness talent, develop skills, empower, and motivate. They must infuse a sense of purpose, encourage teamwork, reward curiosity, award independent thought, provide support, and mediate conflicts. It is the role of the leader to set high expectations and demand extraordinary performance.[1] True leadership is about being a mentor and a coach, creating an environment where people can be at their best.

Being a mentor and coach starts with self-awareness. The leader's strengths, weaknesses, and ability to develop and grow serve as the role model for the organization's employees. Leaders must therefore be what they wish to see in their employees.[2]

The Leader as Mentor: "Mona Lisa"

Mentorship was a grand tradition in the world of art. Artists took on students as apprentices, and the latter learned the craft while assisting the work in the master studio. The method ensured the next generation of accomplished craftsmen and artists. In the traditional master-apprentice relation, they worked side by side, providing hands-on experience. To begin with, apprentices filled what would seem like the minor tasks such as stretching the canvas, and preparing the paints for the master artist. The learning was carried out chiefly along the lines of "watch and do," with the apprentice usually copying the master's work or filling in background areas on the canvas according to instructions given by the master and reflecting the master's style. The intense supervision was crucial to the development of the apprentice.

Numerous works can be ascribed, based on a typical technique and style, to a particular artist's studio. But a discovery of a painting that was preserved in the cellars of the Prado Museum in Madrid sheds additional light on the process of mentorship. The work, discovered in January 2012 and following treatment and cleaning, is a copy of the famous **Mona Lisa** by Leonardo da Vinci (image 28—original, image 29—copy), and art historians assumed that it was produced by one of da Vinci's apprentices. The copy clearly shows good ability with the craft, but it is still considered a pale version of the master's work. It lacks the unique technique and spirit that makes da Vinci's work outstanding. The copy demonstrates the value gained by the apprenticeship. The Mona Lisa copy gives a glimpse into the "human assembly line" of the Renaissance period, but describes the limitations of learning through apprenticeship alone. If apprentice is to do only as the master does, can we expect anything but a pale copy?

Image 28: Leonardo da Vinci, *Mona Lisa*, 1503–1506

Image 29: *Mona Lisa* copy by Da Vinci's apprentice

The Leader as a Coach: To Grow, Like Henri Matisse

In the current business climate, reducing the learner's capability to no more than the mentor's style and experience can limit or inhibit independent thinking and creativity. This highlights the importance of the complementary, and sometimes alternative, coaching approach to employee development. Coaching defines the desired future and the path to realizing it. The role of the leader as coach is to raise the employee's level of awareness, define goals together, and develop the employee's professional and personal skills. As coach, the leader can assist employees in relating to challenges, realizing opportunities, and gaining personal and professional growth. Coaching boosts morality since it contributes to confidence increase, independent thinking, and better teamwork. It is an empowering process, not only to employees and teams, but to the coach as well.

Coaching is very much the method by which art is taught at art academies. It is based on the Socratic method, using questions that will guide the art student to define perceptions, set goals, and defend their ideas and techniques. This process encourages personal and professional growth. To become artists, students need develop a personal vision and convey it in their own unique language. Independent thinking and authentic self-expression are a prerequisite for any artist.

Henri Matisse, among the greats of twentieth-century art, was initially a student and an apprentice in Gustave Moreau's atelier. Observing their work (images 30 and 31) discloses significant stylistic differences. Moreau is involved in mythological and religious themes, and his artistic style matches more that of the academic and rigid style. Matisse, by contrast, rebelled against these traditional norms as a young artist, and sought to develop a new, modern visual language that would express his ideas and vision. Moreau influenced his pupils' personalities by encouraging them to doubt, to question traditional works, to take a stance against what is traditional and accepted. He pushed them to analyze and synthesize ideas, encouraging his pupils to choose their own paths. As Matisse noted of Moreau, "He allowed each of us to gain the techniques that matched our personal temperament." Moreau encouraged his pupils to observe works in the Louvre, to study to understand them, and then embark on their own interpretation. This was a major step in developing one's own personal style.³

As with Matisse, personal coaching helps develop critical thinking. Critical thinking is essential to creative thinking. Only through casting doubt what is, is it possible to imagine what can still be.

Image 30 (Left): Henri Matisse, *Blue Nude III*, 1952

Image 31: Gustave Moreau, *Oedipus and the Sphinx*, 1864

In the modern world, the need for companies to adapt is higher than it has ever been. The current organizational environment is dynamic and diverse. The Western world's Generation Y and the Millennial generation are altering the global work force and setting new leadership challenges. They do not believe in hierarchy, and as far as they are concerned, the world is "flat," in that everything is accessible. Unlike their predecessors, Generation X, the new generations have no patience for climbing the organizational promotions ladder, nor do they position employment stability as a top priority. The gray area of accepting mediocrity belongs, in their minds, to the past, and each of them aspires to express their uniqueness. They operate from the perspective of independent thinking, and prefer self-realization to blind obedience and following traditional norms. Thus the traditional approach of mentoring, where the mentor is basically the sole authority relative to all aspects of knowledge and problem-solving, has pretty much lost its effectiveness and has little impact in the current generation. By contrast, the process of coaching, much like that used in the world of art, may lead employees in a modern generation to greater drive and commitment to the organization while simultaneously allowing for personal growth.

Jack Dorsey has now "inherited" Steve Jobs's title of "the currently most fascinating personality in the hi-tech world." Dorsey, entrepreneur and CEO of the short message network known as Twitter, invests heavily in creating a culture of innovation and creativity in his organization. He does not have an office, a luxurious chair, or an expensive desk. His work is conducted in virtual space at a cluttered table that reminds him of his childhood, where his parents' dining table was the central meeting point for a family that shared experiences, consulted with each other, and enjoyed each other's company.

Dorsey is accessible to his employees, and works alongside them, encouraging them to expand their spheres of interest and to diversify. This helps them develop as individuals and as professionals. In the highly competitive technological world where Dorsey operates, innovation is the name of the game. In his view, innovative ideas surface from among the jumble of thoughts and experiences that may not even seem connected to each other in any way. This is also why he will sit with his employees and watch films together, such as Modern Times by Charlie Chaplin, or Charlie and the Chocolate Factory. In the spacious hall from which Square, the mobile payment pioneer, is run (cofounded by Dorsey), is a recommended reading library holding a broad range of books chosen by Dorsey, his employees, and others.[4]

Leaders in the business world can, like Gustave Moreau or Jack Dorsey, serve more as coaches and less as mentors. In this way, they inspire their employees to grow, learn, and identify their own inherent powers. This is especially true in today's economy where organizations invest great resources to recruit and retain talent. Everyone is looking for intelligent and creative employees. In The Rise of the Creative Class, Richard Florida claims that a plethora of academic research and knowledge exists on developing creativity and innovation in organizations. In the long run, creative individuals and employees in knowledge industries only give their best in organizations with open communication, quality employment conditions, and decency. Employees do not wish to feel as though management has abandoned them to cope alone; on the other hand, they do not work to their best potential under micromanagement or without sufficient autonomy to allow them to think and operate. These employees do not want mechanical instructions but do need some direction. Peter Drucker famously said that employees in knowledge-based industries, unlike those in traditional industries, do not produce better outcomes based on financial incentives, instructions, or sanctions. This led Florida to see the employee in knowledge-based industries as a type of "volunteer," since the greatest satisfaction for volunteers is in the doing itself. Simply put, their motivation for contributing derives from within them.[5]

Although mentoring is an important process of learning, it may result an approximated copy of the mentor's work, such as the Mona Lisa produced by da Vinci's pupil. It is coaching that can bring about the employee's uniqueness and full abilities to light, as it did with Matisse when he developed a new artistic language.

In Short

- Mentoring is a tradition in the art world where apprentices learned by copying masters' work.

- Mentoring alone can lead to pale copies like that of the Mona Lisa.

- Art academies coach students to find their inner voice, like Henry Matisse.

- Coaching encourages growth through empowerment.

- Coaching hones critical thinking, which promotes creativity and innovativeness.

- As a coach, the leader serves as a role model.

PART IV
INFLUENCE

Chapter 10

THE LEADER IS PRESENT

You can have brilliant ideas, but if you can't get them across, your ideas won't get you anywhere.
— Lee Iacocca

In the rapidly changing, complex, and global business arena, communication is one of the most important keys to leadership success. Communication is one of the foundations of trust, which is essential to leading. It is a vehicle to transform vision into inspiration and motivation, and strategies into actions. Communication is about connecting to people, listening to them, sharing ideas and aligning efforts.

Leadership can no longer rely on the formal traditional modes of communication, where the message was passed down from the apex through a pyramidal structure and reflected orders, control, supervision, and review alone. A study conducted over a two-year period, encompassing some 100 midrange and large local and multinational companies and some 150 interviews with top leaders, demonstrated clearly the need for conversation with employees. The study showed that in the current business climate, smart leadership builds direct communication of the kind people are used to for personal discussion. When an organization's communication model includes the culture of conversation, four components develop and blend:

- Intimacy and trust, which allow discourse that promotes intellectual and emotional closeness.

- Interaction and bidirectional communication, via encouragement of employees to express their views on the organization and its leadership, and expose personal challenges. Bidirectional conversation of this kind can help management learn from its employees about real difficulties in the field.

- An orientation toward sharing, creativity, and doing instead of control. Employees become proactive participants in the communication process and thereby contribute to reaching the organization's goals.

- A focus on discourse with employees leading to organizational growth.[1]

Self-image and Influence: Gustav Courbet

Leaders' ability to communicate clearly and powerfully is generally empowered by a positive self-image, confidence, and assertiveness. Self-confidence impacts almost every aspect of the behavior of individuals and leaders. It impacts the ability to influence and persuade, make decisions, deal with failure, and take risks. Self-image and self-confidence are generally apparent and even pronounced in the body language. For leaders, positive self-image and self-confidence are essentials. The body language reflected in the **Self-portrait** of Gustav Courbet could shed light on the importance of the perception of the self. Courbet's image (image 32) is a portrayal of a cocktail of emotions—fright, helplessness, astonishment, and confusion. For the viewer, his image does not offer comfort or trust, but the opposite.

Jamie Dimon, CEO and chair of the banking giant, JP Morgan Chase, is a charismatic and self-confident leader. Dimon led this gargantuan banking concern with

Image 32: Gustav Courbet, *Self-portrait*, 1841

confidence, slicing through the financial crisis that thundered across the banking world in 2008 without any significant losses. In mid-2012, the company blundered into the risky trade known as the "London Whale" affair, losing some $6 billion by making an overly high-risk investment when one of their traders, Bruno Iksil—nicknamed the London Whale on the trading market—gambled on an obscure sector of the credit market.

Dimon stood behind the company's failure, even though he was not the one who made the bad decision. At a congressional hearing in the US, and in umpteen interviews and meetings with the bank's investors, Dimon stood firm as a rock, admitted the error as one point along the way, took overall responsibility as the company's leader, yet continued to express full confidence in the company's investment policies in general, and the company's ability to manage risks. In a talk he gave to investors at a November 2012 company conference in California, he voluntarily asked the audience: "So ask me about the London Whale?" then immediately followed up with fast, confident statements, explaining, "That's it, it's over." He called it a stupid mistake, adding that he definitely takes responsibility, that the company has admitted the error, and primarily, understood it. Based on facts in the field, the company ended Q3 (end of June 2012) with profits up 34 percent. He further explained that the error was not systemic, but a kind of deviation that does not represent the investment strategy of the company. One question directed toward me," he added, "or from any of the company's investment board members concerning delineation and risk management for that investment would have prevented the loss.[2]

Attending that same conference was Lawrence Summers, Treasurer in Bill Clinton's administration, former President of Harvard University, and a member of President Barack Obama's economic steering team. Summers added, "Confidence is the cheapest form of stimulus." Jamie Dimon's solid, direct stance, his standing behind the company, and his taking responsibility derive from true self-confidence combined with his values and position. Dimon's conduct demonstrates that self-confidence is a vital characteristic of the successful leader. It generated authentic stimulus to his employees, managers, and the company's investors. Indeed, analysts in investment markets worldwide expressed their confidence in Dimon's leadership. In a fast-changing world, taking risks cannot be entirely avoided, nor can errors be entirely prevented. But even errors can turn into new opportunities when managed and communicated with confidence and authority.[3]

Present Leadership: A Lesson from Marina Abramovic

Former US President Bill Clinton was known for his outstanding ability to listen to people, to be totally in the present for a moment and allow the person conversing with him the sense of being the most important individual Clinton had ever met. His listening ability empowers those around him and causes them to follow where he leads. True listening is not coincidental, but an honest choice to be present. Listening is a central component of effective interpersonal communication, yet we tend to talk more about ourselves and try to persuade the listener of our views rather than allow for theirs. Active listening involves senses other than hearing. When silence prevails, it becomes possible to hear through the eyes and let the brain listen, too. This kind of listening is what gives the leader the ability to influence.

The Artist is Present is a unique exhibition by the artist Marina Abramovic, held in the New York Museum of Modern Art. The exhibition received unprecedented exposure and showed the power of human connectivity. The performance racked up 750,000 visitors over a three-month show. In the exhibition, Abramovic sat, one-on-one, eight hours a day, every day of the exhibition, in front of viewers who came to the exhibition. Sitting in the large white gallery space, free of any decorative elements, dressed in a long white robe, Abramovic became the "artistic installation." It was a discourse, without any discourse. Museum visitors waited in long lines for a chance to sit facing her for a few minutes, and only very few actually achieved their wish. Some visitors spent the night outdoors waiting for the museum's opening time to be sure they were at the start of the queue for a chance of silent conversation with the artist. Not a word was said, not a gesture made. The only contact between the artist and the person facing her was through gaze. She looked at them silently, flooding them with unexpected emotions.

The effect was dramatic, and sometimes Abramovic herself reacted with tears. No one involved in this silent dialogue remained apathetic to it and its outcomes. Some rose from the seat with smiling faces, or sparkling eyes, while others burst into sobs. The personal, intimate encounter occurred in a hall buzzing with tens of guests watching the event, which was documented and turned into a film.

Marina Abramovic created a charismatic space around the silent discourse. According to the psychoanalyst Jacques Lacan, gazing at another person is part of the longing to complete our own selves. Abramovic succeeded in emotionally and intellectually touching those who sat before her, seeing themselves in her eyes. Her personal strength and her ability to influence derived from the empathy she conveyed through her gaze to the person sitting opposite her. Her authoritative body language, and the direct, attentive eye contact, left no doubt as to the hierarchy of roles and authority in the silent dialogue being created. Abramovic's orientation and direction while gazing at the other gave rise to intimacy and authenticity that caused those sitting opposite her to listen intently to their inner selves.

At the World Economic Forum held in Davos, Switzerland in January 2016, the journalist and author Tom Friedman spoke about leadership and communication. He noted that although the world is becoming increasingly hyper-connected, business organizations still act as though not much has changed. In fact, the power has shifted into the hands of the people and impact increasingly occurs from bottom to top. Although it is common to have direct and constant communication without personal meetings, trust or empathy cannot be "downloaded." There is no substitute for meeting and face-to-face conversation. Personal encounters offer managers the chance to structure their leadership through personal connection and by empowering the employee.

Attentive leadership of this kind is vital in the current hyperlinked age where individuals, whether employees or clients, have a greater impact. Empathic listening, like that used by Marina Abramovic, creates a space that emotionally touches people. In a world where time is an expensive commodity and technology took over, traditional means of communication, the ability to stop for a moment and relate to employees and truly acknowledge their presence can empower and drive motivation and commitment.

The Value of Silence: Joseph Beyus

Silencing of the voice is a central topic in the works of Joseph Beyus. A piano, meant to produce sounds, is wrapped in gray felt (image 33) to represent poetic silence, which is in itself a kind of silent noise. Paradoxically, the musical tool becomes a mute object. In a world where noise is integral to everyday life, silence is a rare commodity. How often have any of us wished to silence the various technological appliances we use for the sake of a few moments of peace and quiet? Beyus turns off the volume of the world people are accustomed to in these modern times, with its technology and electronics, in order to hear and listen to the sound of silence, and perhaps in that way listen to ourselves.

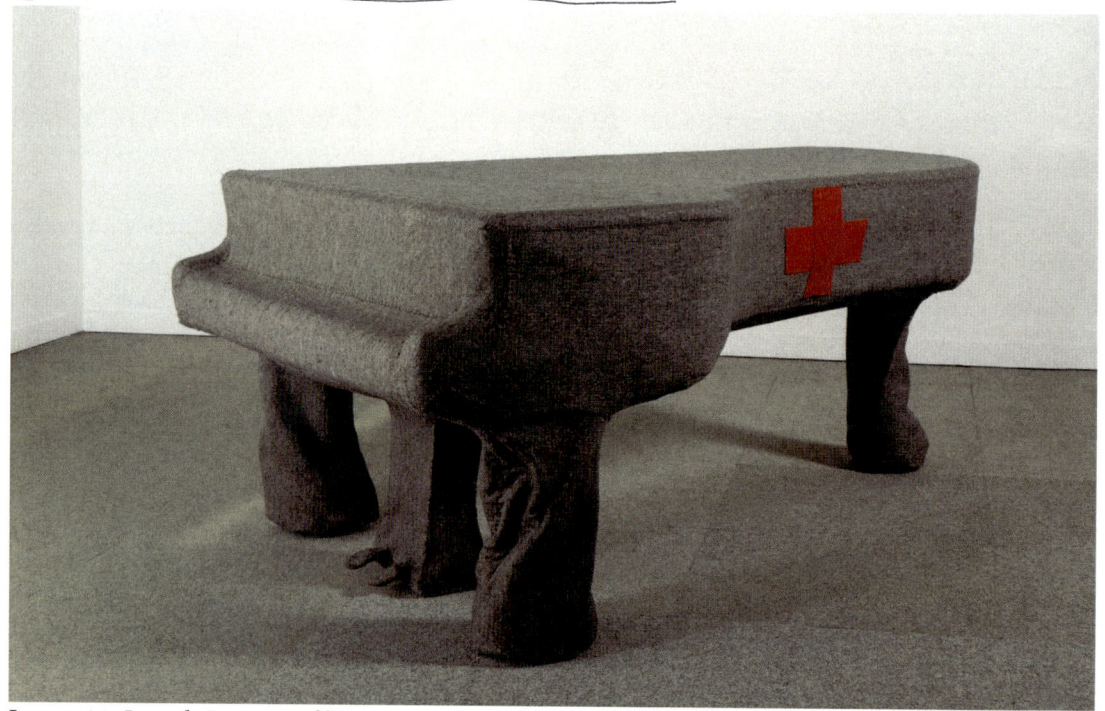

Image 33: Joseph Beyus, *Infiltration-homogen for Grand Piano*, 1966

Silence can allow the leaders to listen to themselves. Jeff Weiner, CEO of LinkedIn, noted in an interview he gave to the New York Times that he devotes between two and three hours every day to thinking and pondering, which lets him see "the full picture."[4]

Time is measured in terms of money in the competitive business world. Managers and leaders are required to achieve more in less time, and demands on their time are constantly on the rise. For this very reason, taking a time-out from regular activities to think and reflect is so important. Pondering allows the brain access to imagination, creating new connections, and chances to look back for the sake of looking forward.

In "The Five Minds of a Manager", coauthored by Henry Mintzberg and Jonathan Gosling and appearing in the Harvard Business Review, the manager's world is presented as burdensome and complex. Integrating different ideas and insights may assist managers in understanding complexity. Managers who do not devote time to understanding their role act more like soldiers on a mission without asking too many questions and may therefore take rash steps. Managers need breathing space, a chance to stop, think, consider. Thinking about the past can lead to setting the future.[5] Silence also allows the leader to listen to others. As Beyus implies, silencing the musical tool can be viewed as a chance to think about how silence can encourage authentic listening. When a musical tool meant to produce sounds is purposely made a mute silent object, it is inherently imbued with new attributes. In the same way, the leader can silence the noise and allow employees to make their voices heard.

Self-Positioning and Branding: Diego Velasquez and the Royal Entourage

Before settling into that well-styled manager's chair, it is worth thinking about how to shape awareness in, and impact on, the target population. Utilizing the new managerial role's opportunity for self-positioning and branding as a charismatic leader able to make others identify with the leader's vision can empower the new manager's impact. Numerous studies indicate the importance of charisma in leaders.

In an article entitled "Learning Charisma: Transform Yourself into the Person Others Want to Follow," appearing in the Harvard Business Review, the authors claim that leaders stand out for their charisma, values, symbols, vision, and verbal and nonverbal communication. Many believe that charisma is an inborn trait that cannot be learned. This is only partially true, and "leadership charisma tactics" can actually be developed. They are drawn from Aristotle's model of influence—logos, ethos, and pathos—which, among several other ways, manifest in communication that uses narrative, anecdote, and metaphor in order to create empathy and express trust in subordinates.[6]

Diego Velasquez uses self-portrait to convey to viewers a narrative of positioning and branding. Velasquez, court artist to Prince Philippe IV of Spain during the seventeenth century, manages to get an overt self-portrait into the painting **Las Meninas**, of Princess Margareta with the royal entourage in a palace hall. In this way, he imbues himself with the status of nobility, as one of the members of the royal court, and a personage of prestige. Other artists, such as Raphael (Raffaello Sanzio da Urbino) or Rembrandt (Rembrandt van Rijn), the renowned Dutch artist of the seventeenth century, embedded their portraits covertly in other works. Of course, this is not a random action but a calculated one with an encoded message relating to their status as "branded" artists of fame and power.

Simply put, a leader's success is influenced by self-image and self-confidence, as proven by Jamie Dimon's balanced handling of the London Whale affair rather than "coming apart at the seams" in the manner of Courbet's self-portrait; by the ability to listen and create a charismatic space, as demonstrated by Marina Abramovic; and by the ability to enter into a state of silence, as manifest in the artistic work of Joseph Beyus. Employees, clients, and all other linked persons are the ones who actually determine the worthiness of a leader to successfully impact, drive, and lead.

In Short

- Communication is the lifeline of leadership.
- Communication builds trust and connects people to a leader's vision.
- Communication is affected by technology and business cultural environment. It obligates a change in an organization's internal communication.
- Leaders can look at artists to:
    » Realize that self-image is evident, as seen in Gustav Courbet's portrait.
    » Self-confidence is an essential to lead and impact, as is seen from Jamie Dimon's behavior.
    » Be present like Marina Abramovic and take time to connect to people face-to-face.
    » Take time for silent pondering and thought, as the work of Beyus and Jeff Wiener shows. It allows new insights to surface, thereby opening up new opportunities.
    » Think about self-positioning and branding, as in Velasquez's work.

Chapter 11

THE ARTIST'S STUDIO: EVALUATION AND FEEDBACK

You are born an original. Don't die a copy.
John L. Mason

Evaluation and feedback are among the most powerful tools available to business managers. An evaluation and feedback conversation helps people attain personal and professional growth and an opportunity to learn something new about them. A personal conversation of this kind drives the employees who are involved in achieving the organization's goals, which in turn reinforces the manager's leadership. Feedback meetings also provide the managers with important information for improving their personal and professional functioning. In a book titled Leadership Alchemy: The Magic of The Leader Coach, the authors claim that the role of leadership is to shape, develop, and acknowledge the team in order to bring it to working independently but fully synchronized with the organization's goals. Leaders, say the authors, need to engage their employees at the emotional and intellectual levels if they are to enjoy the employees' optimal talents and commitment.[1]

The evaluation and feedback process chiefly examines the past as means of impacting the future. Its goal is to communicate with the employee out of sensitivity, sharing processes, setting targets, reinforcing strengths, improving weakness, and implementing insights and conclusions. Evaluation and feedback are wonderful chances for building closeness, mutual understanding, and respect. They are encounters in which the leader can shape achievements, and shape commitment and drive over the long term. Management research and theories have consistently proven beyond doubt that internal-organization tools that promote motivation, such as assessment and feedback discussions, create longer-term impact compared to external tools such as a raise or bonus. In fact, unlike a raise or a promotion, which are not necessarily readily accessible, a feedback conversation can be held as often as needed without significant cost to the organization.

Few dispute the importance of evaluation processes and frequent feedback conversations, but despite the cumulative knowledge concerning their benefits, many managers prefer to "let things be" or grit their teeth prior to conducting such talks. Certainly the fear of descending into "harsh statements" that lead to demotivation deters many managers. But keeping the evaluation and feedback focused on the future, and making a balanced use of intellect and emotion, will strengthen the manager's leadership and empower the employee. Effective feedback is personal, balanced, clear, easy-going in mood, and allows both parties to express themselves through constructive and nonjudgmental manner.

In the art world, evaluation and feedback are fundamental to the artist's development. In fact, the start of this process begins in the art academy, when the teacher and group members provide feedback and assessment at every stage of the creative and artistic activity. Artists in every sphere are open to feedback from peers and viewers. This is not feedback on the artist but on the work. Focus on the product rather than its producer allows listening and containment. In this way the person receiving the feedback can listen and internalize without defensiveness. Indeed, a basic rule in the evaluation and feedback process in art academies is to avoid argument, to pay attention, to relate to what is being said as an opportunity to develop new ideas, and to internalize and implement.[2]

In business, one of the greatest challenges posed by the feedback process is focusing on goals. Openness and readiness to change and enhance personal growth are possible when the dialogue develops without casting blame, but stays within a review of ideas and processes, and how they are implemented, toward improving them. A culture of this kind where feedback helps its recipient to grow and expand professional skills will help consolidate and shape the recipient's professional and personal uniqueness.

The Leader's Unique Voice: The Artist's Studio

In the work titled **The Artist's Studio** (image 34), by the French artist Gustav Courbet, founder of realism and the avant-garde, it is possible to see how the mature artist is working under the influence of feedback. The artist himself is positioned facing the large canvas on its easel. Crowding both sides are two groups of observers. On one side stand members of Courbet's village, simple people with whom he grew up, and on the other side are the intellectual art patrons. The body language of each group narrates their sensations relative to Courbet's work.

The villagers on the left look down and away, and do not seem to be overly interested in the painting. By contrast, the art patrons on the right are presented as showing interest and curiosity, observing with focused attention. Their chins point upward; their faces express analytical thoughts.

Courbet adds three more figures alongside himself in the painting's forward front

Image 34: Gustav Courbet, *The Artist's Studio*, 1855

area: the nude model, a dog, and a child, all standing around him and gazing at the painting. The two groups of observers represent alienation from the painted canvas, while simultaneously accepting the artwork. The child, dog, and nude model, on the other hand, represent the artist's internal voice. The child can be seen as a metaphor for authenticity and naïveté; the dog indicates loyalty, representing the artist's loyalty to his chosen path; and the nude model stands for internal truth. In *The Artist's Studio*, Courbet gives voice to his guiding professional principles. Despite the feedback on his work, or perhaps because of it, he operates out of loyalty, sincerity, and internal veracity.

The process reflected by Gustav Courbet in this work gives expression to one of the most important roles of feedback: a driving factor in consolidation of professional and personal identity. In this age of constant change and uncertainty, organizations need gutsy people with independent views and voices. Effective feedback assists its recipient to develop her or his own "internal professional voice." On occasion, feedback can be a tough experience that feels like it is shredding the work to bits. But the person exiting the end of the tunnel may well have become a finely developed artist. In the business world, this translates into the employee learning to trust her or his skills, develop into an independent worker, be productively self-critical and creative, and learn to identify her or his personal style, unique voice, and ability to be heard clearly.

Feedback and Evaluation: Zoom-in Zoom-out

Visitors to museums tend to move closer to artworks, sometimes coming up real close, "all the better to see them," before taking a few steps back, to look at the "big picture." In this way, the viewer hopes also to catch the brushstrokes, the small details, the textures on the canvas. In works by Georges Seurat, one of twentieth-century art's founding fathers and best-known member of the Pointillist movement, the outcome is the result of a well-thought-out technique. Tightly placed dots of pure color, made by placing the opening of the tube of paint itself directly against the canvas, comprise the painted area. As can be seen in **La Parade** (image 35), these tiny dots connect to form the harmony of the "big picture." Evaluation and feedback in the business world can be considered a kind of Pointillist work, where leaders must relate to multitudinous fine details, yet never lose sight of the fact that the recipient of feedback is part of the whole picture.

Image 35: Georges Seurat, *La Parade*, 1888

Biases: Paul Klee

Biases are methodical and common norms of thought that may lead to erroneous perceptions, memories, and judgments. They generally derive from manifestations of the unconscious. Biases come in various forms, and are sometimes heuristic, functioning to abstract or shorten processes of analysis and thinking, and the time needed for decision-making.

In evaluation and feedback processes, biases are great sins, which influence too many managers. Biases derive from assessor's external sources such as fear, culture, conceptions and opinions, first impressions, herd mentality, or halo effects. Biases impact the feedback's reliability and may therefore express disrespect toward its recipient. Biases also prevent open communication and real chances for growth. It may therefore cause the evaluation conversation to fail while damaging the relationship with the employees and detrimentally affecting their motivation.

Studies on color theory by the Swiss artist Paul Klee, a founder of the Bauhaus Academy, strongly impacted modern art. However, one of his works, titled **Little Hope** (image 36), could easily arouse waves of criticism and ridicule. Reactions of this kind can definitely surface due to lack of appreciation of the concept or aesthetic behind the work or its creator. Often, the source of critical feedback toward abstract works of this kind is based in biases, non-acceptance of difference, non-agreement, and even lack of understanding.

Looking at artworks when discussing biases, fear of difference, and unfounded opposition to the unfamiliar can help open a window on objective dialogue about biases in general, and in feedback discussions in particular. A feedback session, with its many shades and nuances, is an opportunity for all involved to feel they have come

Image 36: Paul Klee, *Little Hope*, 1938

out of a win-win event: the organization, the employees, and the leader alike. Some employees are easier to approach with feedback, since they uphold goals and maintain good communication with their teams and management. Others are more of a challenge, and it is important to hold frequent feedback sessions with them, investing in their personal and professional growth. Either way, the goal of feedback is to promote personal and professional growth among the organization's employees.

In "They're not Employees, They're People," penned by Peter Drucker for the Harvard Business Review, the author claims that the key to excellence is in the inherent potential of each person and developing that potential as far as possible. Statistically, there is a limit to the number of "good" people an organization can recruit. The only way, then, to increase that number is for organizations to develop those qualities in its employees. The challenge is to bring the sum of all employees to excellence. In knowledge-intensive organizations, leadership must invest time in people who show promise by getting to know them, listening to them, challenging and encouraging them. It is equally as important to adopt this approach toward contract workers, even though they are not part of the organization's fixed staff. The people operating in the organization are the primary resource and critical mass capable of ensuring the organization's goals are realized, and as such, they are vital to the organization's success.[3]

In Short

- In the world of art, feedback is one of the foundations for developing independent thinking and personal style.

- Feedback is a highly powerful tool for mutual learning and motivating employees.

- In the info age, the organization aspires to produce and empower employees in order to develop their internal, professional, and personal voice.

- In Peter Drucker's words: leaders should see their employees as people first and foremost.

- Leaders should compose feedback by:

» Seeing the details, but acknowledging the greater picture, like George Seurat.

» Refrain from biases, which are a stumbling block for openness and respect, as seen with the work of Paul Klee.

Chapter 12

CONFLICT MANAGEMENT MIRRORED IN ART

In the middle of difficulty lies opportunity.
Albert Einstein

In all relationships, whether between individuals, groups, organizations, or countries, conflicts do surface. We need to work with people who have different personalities, habits, and values. Naturally, this can be a potential threat, but if managed correctly can actually expand and empower the dialogue. Conflicts are opportunities to transform contrary and divergent views into a creative process that leads to personal and professional growth. In this area too, leaders can learn navigation techniques from artists who set out for new unknowns, since artists by their very nature tend to be unwilling to continue accepting reality as it is. Artists will tend to look at conflicts as a way to challenge themselves, to touch the untouchable issues, testing them for where they can be changed, or where something new can emerge.

Art at its best is the outcome of dialogue and conflict between ideas and materials. The conflict might manifest between the artist and her or his own self, or between ideas and trends accompanying the creative process. The history of art shows that structured conflict catalyzes disruptive or creative innovation. One of the most productive conflicts in art is that of the art academy's traditions and values pitched against the artist's own individualistic language. Artists hold ongoing dialogue with their environments. Their works draw strength and conceptual foundations from the ability to touch and impact. In this sense, art is dynamic, complex, and undefined. By contrast, art studies in an academy attempt to formulate art into definitions, language, meanings, and a scale of values. The eventual collision is the structured conflict that promotes fruitful dialogue and allows the creation of art that is moving and daring.

The business world has always been fertile ground for conflicts. Competition, power, money, and influence together with stakeholders, interests, emotions, opinions, beliefs, and different values creates a charged space. Conflict analysis in organizations shows that often the social structure that is meant to contribute to the company's overall functioning is preferentially beneficial to only some within the organization. It is natural for those with certain advantages to want to preserve their privileges, while others in the organization will be focused on increasing their share of the resource pie.

Conflicts in the twenty-first-century business world are multifaceted. Current organizations face uncertainty and constant change. Employees of the Baby Boomer, Gen-X, and Gen-Y think differently from each other, and the new wave of Millennials is on the verge of entering the marketplace. This mix of generations represents different outlooks and values, which manifest in numerous areas such as dress code, style of speech, perception of their role, attitudes to gender, use of technology, or sharing rather than competing. And all these elements create structured conflict in the business world. Despite the multiple challenges, too many managers avoid coping with the value and personal collisions these differences create, do not relate sufficiently deeply to tough issues, or do not make certain types of decisions for fear of empowering the conflict. They ignore states of non-agreement or tension in the organization, or avoid of decision-making, which can harm the workplace, the leader, and the employees. It is the leader's responsibility to raise difficult questions and to challenge, since it is likely that others will be too guarded to do so. Bringing conflicts to the surface is key to seizing opportunities, empowering employees, and promoting a culture that is creative and open.

Stretching the Shared Line: Barnett Newman

Image 37: Barnett Newman, *Vir Heroicus Sublimis*, 1950

Barnett Newman's art (image 37) titled **Vir Heroicus Sublimis** (Man, heroic and sublime) is a large-scale monochromatic canvas through which a few lines pass. Newman termed them "zips." In his work, Newman wished to express his feelings about the tragic human condition, expressing the spiritual in a simplistic composition. The zips that cross the space and separate its parts actually give the sense of harmony and uniformity. Newman himself used to say that the zip does not cross and divide the painting but the exact opposite.

Organizations can be viewed as Barnett Newman's broad canvas. At first glance, it seems monochromatic and uniform, but a second glance reveals multiple hues. The desire to achieve harmony among the nuanced shades, drawing inward rather than diffusing, is a real leadership challenge. Leadership must make sure Newman's "zip" passes all the way through the organization, unifying and not dividing. In a business organization, this unifying line will run like a silken thread creating open and honest dialogue and connecting the dots between conflicting needs and interests. The dialogue assists in structuring shared values and an organizational culture that respects its partners and leads to creating organizational harmony.

Creating the Harmonious Space: Mark Rothko

Artwork by the Abstract Expressionist artist Mark Rothko (image 38) is typified by shape contraction and abstract rectangular or biomorphic swathes of color. The color of the rectangles and the background is not opaque: fine layers of color layer over each other, hues seeping through each other, mingling and altering the forcefulness of splendor. Edges of each layer are soften and spread to appear as if rotating until the colors seem to lift and hover. It is an effect that imbues Rothko's paintings with depth. The areas of color draw the viewer, inviting her or him to sink into thought, or a kind of meditative state.

The sense of quiet, vibrating harmony in Rothko's works is due to the masterfully placed fine layers of color on each other. Organizations in the business world are, similarly, the sum of the various layers and components. Leadership must seek to create harmony that bases itself on unity but not uniformity. Creative connections among all those involved in the organization is a work of art, a work of masterful handling, whether the layer is employees of different generations, clients, management, or shareholders. Areas such as benefits, attitudes toward authority, upholding schedules, or responsibility for reports are typical sources of conflicts.

Image 38:
Mark Rothko:
Orange, Red, Yellow. 1961

As in Rothko's work, each employee can be viewed as a transparent layer of color that only manifests when all the layers simultaneously coordinate their manifestation. Each layer gives its best, preserving its uniqueness but providing the depth of hue. The harmonious and serene composition is the sum of all its layers. The margins of each layer in the organization should not be contained within a rigid framework. The subdued, trembling edges in Rothko's works create a kind of dynamic, exciting energy. This energy can connect the organization's various layers and encourage creativity and entrepreneurship. When each layer is allowed to leave its mark, new opportunities arise; but the danger of creating chaos also exists. The organization can profit from the rich diversity of its layers only if its leadership invests in linking the values and perceptions of these various worlds into a harmonious fabric. The success of an innovative organization is never dependent on a few people only, but on the entire group of people and the cooperation between them.

Reframing: Roy Lichtenstein

Art teaches how to look again and see things differently in order to create another reality. The works of Roy Lichtenstein, the famous Pop artist, reframe and reposition content. Lichtenstein draws his inspiration from the culture of popular comic books. He paints comics with the paintbrush, imbuing them with a mechanical quality as though produced by printing processes (image 39). Comic books are considered low-level populist culture with a short "expiration date," and as such are not normally exhibited in museums. But Lichtenstein reframes them, turning them into high artistic creation.

Reframing as a concept is also applicable to conflicts' resolution within an organization. Reframing in this context means rethinking the problem, changing the context or content to close the gaps between the objective and subjective, either conscious or unconscious. Different people interpret the same reality differently, based on differences in personality, culture, values, educational levels, and socio-economic levels. Events are perceived from a subjective perspective. It stands to reason, then, that two people simultaneously experiencing the same situation will interpret it in ways that lead to conflict between them. The actual circumstances are often less significant than the interpretation given them.

Reframing conflicts is a creative process to reach creative solutions. Artists such as Lichtenstein seek to remove cognitive obstacles and focus on asking questions about the nature of things as a means of reaching a breakthrough to different modes of thinking. This is also the business leader's mission: reframing conflicts so that new questions about essence and nature of content can be asked so new opportunities can be brought into the open.

Image 39: Roy Lichtenstein. *M-Maybe*…. 1965 © Estate of Roy Lichtenstein

In Short

- In the art world, structured ongoing conflicts empower creativity.

- In the business world, different stakeholders' expectations and intergenerational encounters are fertile ground for conflict development.

- Conflicts are an opportunity for growth.

- Managing conflicts strengthens leadership.

- Leaders can look to solve conflicts by:

    » Drawing a shared line—a "zip"—like that of Barnett Newman.

    » Creating harmonious spaces like those of Mark Rothko.

    » Reframing situations, like Roy Lichtenstein.

Chapter Sources

Preface

1. A previous version, Untitled: Art & Leadership, was published in Hebrew in 2014 by Kinneret, Zmorah-Bitan, Dvir - Publishing House LTD., Israel. I wish to express my appreciation to Seree Zohar for her help in translating the manuscript.

Introduction

1. Conversations with Professor Ronald Heifetz, Co-Founder, Center for Public Leadership, King Hussein bin Talal and Senior Lecturer in Public Leadership, Harvard Kennedy School. April 2017.

Chapter 1

1. Kotter, John. http://blogs.hbr.org/kotter/2013/01/management-is-still-not-leadership.html
2. Heifetz, Ronald A. and Laurie, Donald L. "The Work of Leadership." *Harvard Business Review,* January-February 1997.
3. The Marker Magazine, October 30, 2011.
4. Zenger, John H., Folkman, Joseph R. Sherman, Robert H. Jr. and Steel, Barbara. *How to be exceptional: Drive leadership by magnifying your strengths*. USA: McGraw-Hill Publishers, 2012. Chapter 1: pp. 5–7.
5. Mintzberg, Henry, and Jonathan Gosling. "The Five Minds of a Manager." *Harvard Business Review,* November 2003.
6. Marc, Eldar. I*n Giverny with Claude Monet.* [translated from French] Binyamina Nahar Publishers, 2013, p. 58.

Chapter 2

1. Adler, Nancy. "The Arts & Leadership: Now That We Can Do Anything, What Will We Do?" *Academy of Management Learning & Education,* 2006, Vol. 5, No. 4, 486–499.
2. http://www.damienhirst.com/texts/1996/jan--stuart-morgan
3. Jackson Pollock. "My Painting." Agrinde Publications Ltd. New York (1980), p. 65; originally published in

Possibilities I, New York, Winter 1947–1948. (Jackson Pollock, "My Painting," in Pollock: Painting (edited by Barbara Rose), Agrinde Publications Ltd: New York (1980), p. 65; originally published in *Possibilities I,* New York, Winter 1947–1948).

4. Vance, Ashlee. "Facebook Tops 1,000,000,000 Users." *Bloomberg Business Week*, April 10, 2012.
5. Bell, Katherine. "The MFA Is the New MBA." *Harvard Business Review,* April 14, 2008.
6. Orpaz, Inbal. "Modu's Big Bang: The company is dead—30 startups are born." *The Marker Financial News,* July 11, 2013.

Chapter 3

1. Conversations with Professor Ronald Heifetz, Co-Founder, Center for Public Leadership, King Hussein bin Talal and Senior Lecturer in Public Leadership, Harvard Kennedy School. April 2017.Conversations with Professor Ronald Heifetz, Co-Founder, Center for Public Leadership, King Hussein bin Talal and Senior Lecturer in Public Leadership, Harvard Kennedy School. April 2017.
2. Goleman, Daniel, Richard Boyatzis, and Annie McKee. *Primal Leadership.* New York: Harvard Business Review Press, 2008. pp. 105–109.
3. Edersheim, Elizabeth Haas. T*he Definitive Drucker.* New York: McGraw-Hill, 2007. p. 198.

Chapter 4

1. Novak, David. *Taking People With You.* New York: Penguin Group, 2012.
2. Hansen, T. Morten, Ibarra, Herminia, Peyer, Urs. "100 Best Performing CEOs in the World." *Harvard Business Review,* January-February, 2013.
3. World Economic Forum, Davos, Switzerland, 2015.
4. Anderlini, Jamil, "Person of the Year." *Financial Times,* December 13, 2013.
5. https://www.virgin.com/richard-branson/ba-cant-get-it-up-best-stunt-ever
6. Van Gogh, Vincent. The Complete Letters of Vincent Van Gogh. 2nd ed., Vol. 1–3. Greenwich, Ct.: New York Graphic Society, NY, 1959. 3:420.

Chapter 5

1. http://unstats.un.org/unsd/gender/chapter4/chapter4.html
2. Dexter, Emma and Tanya Barsons, Eds. Frida Kahlo. London: Tate Publishing, 2005: 31.
3. Biron, Michal, Rene De Reuver, and Sharon Toker. "All employees are equal, but some are more equal than others: dominance, agreeableness, and status inconsistency among men and women." European Journal of Work and Organizational Psychology Journal, volume 25, 2016—issue 3, pp. 430–446.
4. Sandberg, Sheryl. Bernard College Commencement. New York, May 17, 2012

Chapter 6

1. Collins, James C. and Jerry I. Porras. Built To Last, Successful Habits of Visionary Companies. New York: Harpers Business Books, 2002, p. 241.
2. Fried, Jason. Some advice from Jeff Bezos. Interview at 37Signal.com, October 19, 2012.
3. Stevens, Mark. Extreme Management. London: Harper Collins Business, pp. 58–59.
4. JPMorgan CEO Summit. Napa Valley, California, November 8, 2012.
5. Krames, Jeffrey A. What the Best CEOs Know. New York: McGraw-Hill, 2004. pp. 137–138.

Chapter 7

1. World Economic Forum, Davos, Switzerland, 2014.
2. Govindarajan, Vijay and Chris Timble. "The CEO's Role in Business Model Reinvention." Harvard Business Review. January-February 2011. pp. 109–114.
3. Stewart, James B. Behind eBay's Comeback. New York Times, July 27, 2012.
4. World Economic Forum, Davos, Switzerland, 2013..
5. Conversations with Professor Ronald Heifetz, Co-Founder, Center for Public Leadership, King Hussein bin Talal and Senior Lecturer in Public Leadership, Harvard Kennedy School. April 2017.

Chapter 8

1. Drucker, Peter F., The Age of Discontinuity. New York: Harper & Row, 1968, pp. 246.
2. Gates, William III, Business @ The Speed of Thought. New York: Warner Books Inc. 1999, pp. 187.

3. Jaruzelsky, Barry, John Loehr, and Richard Holman. The 2013 Global Innovation 1000 Study: Navigating the digital future. www.boozallen.com
4. Stevens, Mark. Extreme Management. London: Harper Collins Business, 2001, pp. 50.
5. Drucker, Peter F. "The Discipline of Innovation." Harvard Business Review, August 2002, pp. 46.
6. Blum, Sophie. www.pgisrael.co.il/innovationstrategy
7. Galenson, David W. Conceptual Revolutions in Twentieth Century Art. New York: Cambridge University Press, 2009, pp. 11–15.
8. Drucker, Peter F. "The Discipline of Innovation." Harvard Business Review, August 2002, pp. 42.
9. Donahoe, John. JPM CEO Summit, Napa Valley, California: November 8, 2012.
10. Conversations with Professor Ronald Heifetz, Co-Founder, Center for Public Leadership, King Hussein bin Talal and Senior Lecturer in Public Leadership, Harvard Kennedy School. April 2017.

Chapter 9

1. "The Leader as a Coach." www.toastmasters.org/members
2. Toastmasters International, Item 318A, May 2011.
3. Whitefield, Sarah. Fauvism. London: Thames & Hudson, 1966: 28.
4. "Simplicity and Order for All." Innovator of the Year in Technology 2012. New York, November 8, 2012.
5. Florida, Richard. The Rise of the Creative Class (revisited). New York: Basic Books, 2012: pp. 113–114.

Chapter 10

1. Groysberg, Boris and Michael Slind. "Leadership is a Conversation: How to Improve Employee Engagement and Alignment in Today's Flatter, More Networked Organizations." Harvard Business Review, June 2012: pp. 77–84.
2. JPMorgan CEO Summit. Napa Valley, California: November 8, 2012.
3. ibid.
4. Bryant, Adam. "In Sports or Business, Always Prepare for the Next Play." New York Times, November 10, 2012.
5. Mintzberg, Henry and Jonathan Gosling. "The Five Minds of a Manager." Harvard Business Review, November 2003: pp. 56–59.

6. Antonakis, John, Marika Fenley, and Sue Liechti. "Learning Charisma: Transform Yourself into the Person Others Want to Follow," Harvard Business Review, June 2012: pp. 127–130.

Chapter 11

1. Wright, S. and C. MacKinnon. "Leadership Alchemy: The Magic of The Leader Coach." TCP Publications, Toronto, 2003: pp. 121-122.
2. Bell, Katherine. "The MFA Is the New MBA." Harvard Business Review blog. April 2008. http://blogs.hbr.org/2008/04/the-mfa-is-the-new-mba/
3. Drucker, Peter. "They're Not Employees, They're People." Harvard Business Review, February 2002: pp. 64–68.

List of Images and Artwork Credits

Chapter 1

1. Claude Monet, *Water Lilies*, 1919.
   Metropolitan Museum of Art, New York / The Walter H. and Leonore Annenberg Collection, Gift of Walter H. and Leonore Annenberg, 1998, Bequest of Walter H. Annenberg, 2002.

Chapter 2

2. Damien Hirst, *Anatomy of an Angel*, 2008.
   © Damien Hirst and Science Ltd., All rights reserved, DACS 2017.

3. Méret Oppenheim, *Spoon, Saucer, Fur Cup*, 1936.
   MOMA, New York / Spoon, Saucer, Fur Cup, Oppenheim Méret © 2016, ProLitteris, Zurich. TopFoto.co.uk / ASAP Creative.

4. Édouard Manet, *Portrait of Emil Zola*, 1868.
   Musée d'Orsay, Paris, France / Giraudon / The Bridgeman Art Library / ASAP Creative

Chapter 3

5. Michael Drucks, *Druksland*, 1974–1975.
   From Flexible Geography (My Atlas) 1971-1979, screen-print, 34 x 43 cm'. Courtesy of Tel Aviv Museum / Gift of Gordon Gallery.

6. Barbara Kruger, *Untitled (I Buy Therefore I Am)*, 1987.
   Barbara Kruger, *Untitled* (I buy therefore I am), 111" by 113" (282 cm by 287 cm), photographic silkscreen/vinyl, 1987. © Barbara Kruger. Courtesy: Mary Boone Gallery, New York.

Chapter 4

7. Edvard Munch, *Self-Portrait with Cigarette*, 1985.
   Nasjonal Galleriet, Oslo, Norway / The Bridgeman Art Library / ASAP Creative.

8. Edvard Munch, *The Scream*, 1893.
   Nasjonal Galleriet, Oslo, Norway / The Bridgeman Art Library/ ASAP Creative.

9. René Magritte, *The Clairvoyant*, 1936.
   Private Collection / Magritte René, *The Clairvoyance*, 1936, © ADAGP, Paris 2016 and © Succession René Magritte ADAGP, Paris 2014. Private Digitale (A), Coll. Huile sur toile © 2014. BI, ADAGP, Paris/Scala, Florence.

10. René Magritte, *The Treachery of Images*, 1929.
    Private Collection / Magritte René, *The Treachery of Images*, 1935 © ADAGP, Paris 2016 and © Succession René Magritte / ADAGP, Paris 2016. | Akg-images / ASAP Creative.

11. Jacques Louis David, *Napoleon Crossing St. Bernard*, 1800.
    Château de Malmaison, Rueil-Malmaison, France / Akg-images / ASAP Creative.

Chapter 5

12. Cindy Sherman, *Untitled #92*, 1981.
    Cindy Sherman, *Untitled # 92*, Chromogenic color print, 61X 121.9 cm, The Museum of Modern Art, Courtesy of the artist and Metro Pictures.

13. Barbara Kruger, *Untitled (Your Body is a Battleground)*, 1989.
    Barbara Kruger, Untitled (Your body is a battleground), 112" by 112" (284.5 cm by 284.5 cm), photographic silkscreen/vinyl, 1989 © Barbara Kruger. Collection: The Broad Art Museum, Los Angeles, California. Courtesy: © Mary Boone Gallery, New York.

Chapter 6

14. Gustave Moreau, *Oedipus and the Sphinx,* 1864.
    Metropolitan Museum of Art, New York / Gift of Herman and Lila Shickman, and Purchase, Lila Acheson Wallace Gift, 1997.

15. Édouard Manet, *Olympia*, 1863.
    Musée d'Orsay, Paris, France / Giraudon / The Bridgeman Art Library / ASAP Creative.

16. Titian, *Venus of Urbino*, 1538.
    Galleria degli Uffizi, Florence, Italy / The Bridgeman Art Library / ASAP Creative.

Chapter 7

17. Pablo Picasso, *The Artist Mother*, 1896.
    Pablo Picasso, *Violin*, © Succession Picasso 2017, The Bridgeman Art Library / ASAP Creative.

18. Pablo Picasso, *Self-Portrait*, 1907.
    Pablo Picasso, *Self-Portrait*. © Succession Picasso 2017. Národní Galerie, Prague, Czech Republic / Giraudon / The Bridgeman Art Library / ASAP Creative.

19. Pablo Picasso, *Violin*, 1912.
    Pablo Picasso, *Violin*, © Succession Picasso 2017, The Pushkin Museum of Art, Moscow. Akg-images / ASAP Creative.

20. Pablo Picasso, *Portrait of Sylvette 1*, 1954.
    Pablo Picasso, Portrait of Sylvette, © Succession Picasso 2017. Private Collection / Giraudon / TheBridgeman Art Library / ASAP Creative.

21. Pablo Picasso, *Portrait of Sylvette David in a Green Armchair*, 1954.
    Pablo Picasso, *Sylvette David in Green Armchair,* © Succession Picasso 2017. Private Collection / Photo © Christie's Images / The Bridgeman Art Library / ASAP Creative.

Chapter 8

22. Henri Matisse, *Woman with a Hat*, 1905.
    © Succession H. Matisse / Photo San Francisco Museum of Modern Art, bequest of Elise S. Haas.

23. Piet Mondrian, *Composition*, 1923.
    Metropolitan Museum of Art, New York / Jacques and Natasha Gelman Collection, 1998.

24. Marcel Duchamp, *Fountain*, 1917.
    © ADAGP, Paris 2016 and © Succession Duchamp Marcel / ADAGP, Paris 2016. The Israel Museum, Jerusalem, Israel / Vera & Arturo Schwarz Collection of Dada and Surrealist Art / The Bridgeman Art Library / ASAP Creative.

25. Christo, *Wrapped Reichstag*, 1995.
    Courtesy and Photo: Wolfgang Volz. © Christo 1995–2005.

26. Andy Warhol, *Campbell's Soup Cans*, 1968.
    © 2016 The Andy Warhol Foundation for the Visual Arts, Inc. / Artists Rights Society (ARS), New York. Private Collection / The Bridgeman Art Library / ASAP Creative.

27. Erwin Wurm, *House Attack*, 2006.
   Mixed media, 5 x 10 x 7 m, Courtesy: Galerie Thaddeus Ropac, Salzburg (A), Paris (F), Photo © Lisa Rastl.

Chapter 9

28. Leonardo da Vinci, *Mona Lisa*, 1503–1506.
   Louvre, Paris, France / Giraudon / The Bridgeman Art Library / ASAP Creative.

29. Unknown, *Mona Lisa*.
   © Museo Nacional del Prado, Madrid, Spain.

30. Henri Matisse, *Blue Nude III*, 1952.
   © Succession H. Matisse / Photo Musée National d'Art Moderne, Centre Pompidou, Paris, France.

31. Gustave Moreau, *Oedipus and the Sphinx*, 1864.
   Metropolian Museum of Art, New York / Bequest of William H. Herriman, 1920.

Chapter 10

32. Gustav Courbet, *Self-Portrait*, 1841.
   Private Collection / Akg-images / Archives CDA / ASAP Creative.

33. Joseph Beyus, *Inflitration-Homogen for Grand Piano*, 1966.
   Beuys Joseph, © ADAGP, Localisation : Paris, Musée National d'Art Moderne - Centre Georges Pompidou © Centre Pompidou, MNAM-CCI, Dist. RMN-Grand Palais / Adam Rzepka.

Chapter 11

34. Gustav Courbet, *The Artist Studio*, 1955.
   Musée d'Orsay, Paris, France / Akg-images / Maurice Babey / ASAP Creative.

35. George Seurat, *La Parade*, 1888.
   Metropolitan Museum, New York / Bequest of Stephen C. Clark, 1960.

36. Paul Klee, *Little Hope,* 1938.
   Metropolitan Museum of Art, New York / The Berggruen Klee Collection, 1984

Chapter 12

37. Barnett Newman, *Vir Heroicus Sublimis*, 1950-1951.
    Newman, Barnett: Vir Heroicus Sublimis, 1950–1951. 10 x 12 (1)(A) Oil on canvas, 7' 11 3/8' x 17' 9 1/4' (242.2 x 541.7 cm). Gift of Mr. and Mrs. Ben Heller. Acc. n.: 240.1969. Courtesy of The Barnett Newman Foundation © 2016 Digital image, The Museum of Modern Art, New York/Scala, Florence.

38. Mark Rothko, *Orange, Red*, Yellow, 1958.
    © 1998 Kate Rothko Prizel & Christopher Rothko / Artists Rights Society (ARS), New York. Private Collection / Photo © Christie's Images / The Bridgeman Art Library / ASAP Creative.

39. Roy Lichtenstein, *M-Maybe…*, 1965
    Museum Ludwig, Cologne, Germany / Courtesy of © Estate of Roy Lichtenstein. Akg-images / ASAP Creative.